THE EARLY POETRY OF ROBERT GRAVES

Literary Modernism Series
Thomas F. Staley, Editor

THE EARLY POETRY OF
ROBERT GRAVES

THE GODDESS BECKONS

FRANK L. KERSNOWSKI

University of Texas Press, Austin

First edition, 2002

Requests for permission to reproduce material from this work should be sent
to Permissions, University of Texas Press, Box 7819, Austin, TX 78713-7819.

ⓧ The paper used in this book meets the minimum requirements of
ANSI/NISO Z39.48-1992 (R1997) (Permanence of Paper).

Library of Congress Cataloging-in-Publication Data

Kersnowski, Frank L., 1934–
The Early Poetry of Robert Graves : The Goddess Beckons / Frank L.
Kersnowski.— 1st ed.
    p.   cm.—(Literary modernism series)
Includes bibliographical references and index.
ISBN 978-0-292-72365-8
1. Graves, Robert, 1895– 2. Graves, Robert, 1895– —Childhood and
youth. 3. Authors, English—20th century—Biography. 4. World War,
1914–1918—Veterans—Biography. 5. Modernism (Literature)—Great
Britain. 6. Soldiers—Great Britain—Biography. 7. War neuroses—
Patients—Biography. I. Title. II. Series.
PR6013.R35 Z729 2002
821'.912—dc21
[B]   2001053192

This book is for Alice

Lovers and madmen have such seething brains
Such shaping fantasies, that apprehend
More than cool reason ever comprehends.
The lunatic, the lover, and the poet
Are of imagination all compact
One sees more devils than vast hell can hold:
That is the madman. The lover, all as frantic,
Sees Helen's beauty in a brow of Egypt.
The poet's eye, in a fine frenzy rolling,
Doth glance from heaven to earth, from earth to
    heaven:
And as imagination bodies forth
The forms of things unknown, the poet's pen
Turns them to shapes, and gives airy-nothing
A local habitation and name.
Such tricks hath strong imagination
That, if it would but apprehend some joy,
It comprehends some bringer of that joy;
Or in the night, imagining some fear,
How easy is a bush supposed a bear!

A Midsummer Night's Dream (V:I:4–22)

CONTENTS

PREFACE

The Argument

Robert Graves lived an exciting life. Before he was twenty, he was an officer in the Royal Welch Fusiliers. Before he was thirty, he had fought in the Great War with honor, was familiar with the most important political and literary figures of his time, and had written poetry and critical studies that had brought him fame if not money. Then, in the midst of personal scandal, he abandoned England and moved to a rural village on Mallorca, one of the Balearic Islands. Forced to leave by the outbreak of the Spanish Civil War, he was rootless until he returned in 1950. By then he had written historical novels of great distinction and popularity, and had contributed two phrases to *Bartlett's Book of Familiar Quotations:* "Good-Bye To All That" and "The White Goddess." He had renewed his friendship with T. S. Eliot, who published *The White Goddess.* He had also gained the animosity of Ezra Pound, which he returned in kind. W. H. Auden had become an admirer; Graves would follow him as Oxford Professor of Poetry. From the time of his return to Mallorca until his death, Graves constantly received the adulation of visitors both unknown and known to all the world. Schemes were offered to him by financiers, media moguls, and crooks. He raised two families of four children each, intriguing and consequential families. His writing might never have gone beyond memoirs and a fictionalized life. His own everyday life (exciting as it was) only entered his writing in the most oblique ways. That life has so fascinated his critics that they have worried at it for years, virtually to the exclusion of the writings. Yet no one would be interested in Robert Graves if he had not been among those who shaped twentieth-century literature.

What follows here is a study of the birth and development of Graves's poetic self and talent, which were inseparable and often not evident in the day-to-day life made public by his biographers. Graves very early made his poetry into an experience of its own, one informed by his psychological and spiritual discoveries. These began with the experience of World War I and his wounds, not only those which almost killed him but also those which caused what he called his "war neurosis." Such disorientation, hauntings, and compulsiveness were recorded by innumerable writers and artists, from Hemingway and cummings to Sassoon and Graves among the Allies. Their opponents told similar tales of being estranged from life without war while being terrified by war, of being brave and afraid. What makes these writers different from one another is not their experiences, but their reactions to those experiences.

For Graves, the trauma inflicted by war opened a door into the unconscious. Though not an exceptional occurrence, since World War I gave birth to the widespread practice of modern psychiatry, what Graves found within made unusual sense of what was without: love, passion, violence, unpredictability. His writing, especially the poetry, records and celebrates his accommodating such powers. In so doing, he rejected the essential components of the Western idea of reality: reason and predictability, the heritage of Aristotle and the glory that was Greece. Unpredictability, especially, he made a characteristic of the White Goddess, deifying what he could not control.

The void was filled by his respect for his own life as it was given to him by woman or by a woman, initially his wife Nancy Nicholson. He made her responsible for his health and sanity. In time, he would see both himself and his devotion to a woman as necessary for his spiritual awareness and, unquestionably, for his poetry. Woman as muse was representative of an awesome and almost indescribable power. The spirit that informs his early poetry is the unfamiliar, the other. In the forties, he gave the spirit a name, "the White Goddess," though in a poem published in 1924, "A History," he called this spirit "the death-white Fay." Graves saw the feminine as the fundamental force in life, both in his personal life and in the life of the culture. He would claim matriarchy as the basic form of society, the goddess as the all-powerful deity, and his life as poet and scholar driven by the purpose of celebrating and explaining the matriarchy and its deity.

Perhaps Graves's biography could be written from such a perspective, but it has not been. The tracking and equating of the details of his life with his spiritual commitment would strain any scholar's talent and the credibility of any reader. Though one could, without difficulty, show the effects of his worship in all his serious relationships with women, too much of interest would be omitted, including his friendships with Edward Marsh, Winston Churchill, T. E. Lawrence, and John Buchan, to mention a few.

But without his worship of the Goddess, both Graves and his writing would have lacked direction and force.

In this study I examine the growth of Graves's spiritual and poetic awareness from his first volume, *Over the Brazier*, to *Poems (1914–1926)*. During this discrete time, his course as poet and lover was set. Though he would respond to many changes in his life and to many new forces, he would hold to the poetic he established at this time: English, mystical, and Romantic. He did not come forth full-blown from the head of the Goddess, however, but grew slowly into his awareness, and part of the problem in understanding his development is to be able to treat discursively what seems an inseparable whole: emotion, intellect, and spirit all tangled together like a bag full of fish hooks. To pick out one is to draw out many. So I have dumped the bag onto my desk and separated the pieces. In this I was fortunate to have as guide Shakespeare's Theseus, who was also troubled by the similarities among lunatics, lovers, and poets. The story I tell is of a young man driven so mad by the moon that he made her into the heavenly body by which he steered his life. Yet only his poetry tells the tale.

All parts of Graves's life were touched by this story that, later, he would say is the only one worth telling. To place Graves in context, I offer selective, not comprehensive, biographical information, lest his exciting everyday life supplant the spiritual tale. Thus, I have restricted myself, when possible, to his relationships with people central to his poetic life. I have chosen Edward Marsh, Siegfried Sassoon, and Nancy Nicholson, his closest confidants. I have looked closely at selected poems in manuscript to let the explication tell the tale by significant example rather than by repetition. I have looked at the first published versions of the poems, not his revisions. He revised constantly, changing poems in structure and content to agree with his own changing poetic. And, finally, I have looked at the still shocking reality of his poetry.

ACKNOWLEDGMENTS

Beryl Graves's reading of an early draft of this book and her encouragement and comments have done much to give it shape; errors in judgment may well have occurred when I was not assiduous in following her advice. Catherine Nicholson Dalton has been generous with information about her mother, Nancy Nicholson, and I am indebted to her for reading a late draft. Readings by John Presley, Phillip Herring, David Edwards, and Tom Staley have been extremely helpful. Understandings in matters of interpretation have come from Alice Hughes, John Presley, C. W. Spinks, William Walker, and Dunstan Ward. And Alice Hughes has been constant in discussion of all matters concerning Graves and literature of the twentieth century. I am especially grateful to William Graves for his advice, support, and friendship. I must, as well, mention Alexis Mills, who has done much to separate the wheat from the chaff of my prose.

Quotations from Robert Graves's published work and from unpublished manuscripts appear here with the permission of the A. P. Watt Ltd. and Carcanet Press on behalf of the Robert Graves Copyright Trust, the Berg Collection at the New York Public Library, the Modern Poetry Collection at the State University of New York at Buffalo, Special Collections of Southern Illinois University at Carbondale, and the Harry Ransom Humanities Research Center at the University of Texas at Austin. The photographs of Robert Graves, his family, Siegfried Sassoon, and Edward Marsh are from the Canneluñ Archive and are published here with the permission of the Robert Graves Trust. Quotations from Catherine Dalton's letters appear here with her permission. Reference to the letter from Carl Jung to Lawrence Durrell is included with permission from Special Collections of Southern Illinois University at Carbondale. Quotation from a reflection on Graves by H. E. Palmer appears with permission from the Harry Ransom Humanities Research Center of the University of Texas at

Austin. Quotations from *Siegfried Sassoon Diaries* appear with permission from Faber and Faber, and quotations from his *Complete Poems* and *The Complete Memoirs of George Sherston* appear with permission from the Barbara Levy Literary Agency.

Parts of this book have appeared as "'Sullen Moods': From Extant Drafts to Completed Poem" (*Gravesiana* 1:4 [December 1997]) and as "Traumas of Love and Death: Early Signs of the Goddess" (*Graves and the Goddess: Essays on Robert Graves*, Association of University Presses, 2001) and are incorporated into this book with the permission of the editors, respectively Ian Firla and Patrick Quinn.

I am greatly indebted to Shelley Cox of Special Collections at Southern Illinois University at Carbondale; to Robert Bertholf of the Modern Poetry/Special Collection at the State University of New York at Buffalo; to Tom Staley of the Humanities Research Center at the University of Texas; and to Stephen Crook and Philip Milito of the Berg Collection at the New York Public Library.

THE EARLY POETRY OF ROBERT GRAVES

CHAPTER I

THE LUNATIC, THE LOVER, AND THE POET

The Sibyl

Her hand falls helpless: thought amazements fly
Far overhead, they leave no record mark—
Wild swans urged whistling across dazzled sky,
Or Gabriel hounds in chorus through the dark
Yet when she prophesies, each spirit swan,
Each spectral hound from memory's windy zones,
Flies back to inspire one limb-strewn skeleton
Of thousands in her valley of dry bones.

There as those life-restored battalions shout
Succession flags and Time goes maimed in flight:
From each live gullet twenty swans glide out
With hell-packs loathlier yet to amaze the night.

Whipperginny

My friendship with Robert Graves was actually interrupted by meeting him. When I first wrote to him in 1969, I had gone well beyond the obligatory reading of his most recent *Collected Poems* (1961) and *The White Goddess,* having sought out such, then, rare works as *Over the Brazier,* his first volume of poetry, and very recent works, such as *Mammon and the Black Goddess* and *The Rubaiyat of Omar Khayyam,* both of which Robert Graves signed for me. But I had not yet read the accumulating letters and manuscripts in university libraries, nor had I seen reason to be concerned with that part of his life Graves described as "unpublishable" in his afterword to the revised edition of *Good-Bye To All That* (1957). I wrote to him believing that the presence of the man would lead me through the maze of myth and history of his writings into the light and darkness of his creative self. I was mistaken.

My interest became that of a pilgrim when Graves replied to a letter I wrote almost whimsically and with as much expectation of a reply as I have of suddenly acquiring great wealth. The letter I received is on the opposite page, reflective and warm, a very personal response to a complete stranger. Perhaps he replied to many in the same way. I knew that a few years before a friend of mine had also written for an audience and had gone to see Graves at his home in Deya on the island of Mallorca only to be turned away. I was speechless when Robert invited me into his study with: "Anyone who has anything to say is always welcome in my house." Speech recovered, I stammered out questions about the Persian saddlebags draped over the chest on which I sat and so began a conversation about rugs, poems, and friends:

> About the rug under his desk: "Do you know who sheared the sheep, spun the wool, wove the rug? . . . Ben Gurion." About another rug: "There's one upstairs you must see." We almost raced up the stairs, as Robert chatted about this and that: "We'll walk to the village and see if my friends from France have left."
>
> So as I stood on another rug that was probably made close to the Caucusus, Robert Graves changed into his walking shorts. A poet as accomplished and as important as any in this century stood in front of me in his white boxer underwear, chatting away. Certainly unexpected and perhaps inappropriate, his behavior was unpremeditated, unreflective, and utterly unindicative of his writing. (*Conversations* 73–76)

As we talked, he told me of what he had ten years before termed "unpublishable": "I was a virgin until I was married and was never with another woman until my wife forced me to. I left with that woman, and my wife left with her husband." The story of that period in his life has been told by Martin Seymour-Smith, Richard Perceval Graves, and Miranda Seymour in greater detail than is of interest or significance to me. I was not, in fact, concerned with what Robert told me or I would have published an unguarded remark as gossip in the costume of literary criticism. I saw no reason to write about my visit until his biographers had revealed more than he probably remembered, and I do so now only to indicate that Graves's affairs and battles tell a story that too often distracts from Graves's complex creativity.

In 1925 Robert Graves and his wife Nancy Nicholson invited the American poet Laura Riding to visit them. She arrived in England on

Easter
Sunday

Deyá
Mallorca
Spain

Dear Frank Kersnowski:

I saw John Montague in Paris about a fortnight ago — I was talking on the radio about my Brythonic Greeks — & liked him very much

I will be here all summer so far as I know.

Am I the last of the Anglo-Irish poets? Well maybe. Our family went to Ireland in 1575 and I still retain the family's respect for "English as they speak it in Ireland" which means with correctitude and love.

My most recent poems are Poems About Love , Doubleday ; Poems 1965-8 Cassell ; and Beyond Giving limited edition in a few weeks published by Bertram Rota

Saxon Hills, London W.1
I know in contemporary poets but Montague & Seamus Heaney — but Kinsella of New Writers
All the best Robert Graves

Letter from Robert Graves to Frank Kersnowski

2 January 1926 and left there—with Nancy, Graves, and their children—for Egypt on 9 January (Seymour-Smith 129). She and Graves were collaborators and soon lovers, with Nancy as part of the ménage à trois. The addition of Geoffrey Phibbs added even more difficulties to an already tense situation. Phibbs's lack of faith in Riding's philosophical views and his preference for Nancy Nicholson created great stress for Riding, who insisted on her unchallenged authority. When Phibbs made clear he was leaving with Nicholson, Riding stepped out of the window of a fourth-story flat and broke her back. As Robert and Nancy's daughter Catherine Dalton told me in May of 2000, Riding had tried to persuade her, then six years old, to step out the same window, saying steps would appear and she could go up to a garden. Graves jumped out after her from the third story. She lived, and he was only slightly injured. Nicholson and Phibbs left together with the four children, and Riding and Graves moved to Mallorca on the suggestion of Gertrude Stein. They lived platonically with each other on the island until 1936, when the Spanish Civil War necessitated their departure. By 1939 they had moved to New Hope, Pennsylvania, at the invitation of T. S. Matthews. There Riding developed a passion for Schyler Jackson. His wife, Kitty, suffered extreme psychological trauma, or in the words of Martin Seymour-Smith, she went "mad" in 1939. No one likes to talk about them. Laura Riding (so it would appear to an outsider) came to England in 1926 and broke up a family consisting of a wife and husband and four children, and Seymour-Smith's summary of "the happenings at New Hope, Pennsylvania," seems a good one:

> When she came back to her own country (a prophet, and as yet honoured only by a few lines in *Time,* which she apparently did not repudiate when it had an initial capital), she broke up another family also consisting of a wife and husband and four children. But it is possible that she has been misjudged, that she acted for "the general good," a phrase which, like "the general honour," she is fond of using. (331)

While I was in Deya, walking to the post office with Graves or helping him make jam seemed normal, as did seeing him chortle while his wife Beryl ordered me to carry in a case of wine because Robert had hurt his back, or seeing him dive into the Mediterranean from a stone outcrop. Away from Deya's cafes, the *calle* that led to the cove, in the openness of the Graves's kitchen, and back in touch with the books written by Graves, I once again met the friend who had turned my fears and dreams into poetry and prose that stunned with its force and accuracy, as in "The Pier-Glass," that early poem of the succubus:

> Lost manor where I walk continually
> A ghost, while yet in woman's flesh and blood. (14)

Perhaps I should have asked where he saw her: in his mind's eye or in his house. I didn't, having found such questions produced extraneous responses. Anyway, I had not come to footnote the poems, and I believe Graves knew my reason for being there was to find out what had drawn me there.

Graves's early assertion in *Poetic Unreason* (1925)—"The appreciation of Poetry presupposes a common interest or group of interests between the poet and his reader" (2–3)—suggests that having lunch with him might lead to greater understanding of those "interests"—or so I hoped. Yet I knew that he also believed what he had written later in the same book: that even when the poet is anonymous, we know the essentials of the life: "politics, culture, nationality, his attitude to war, to love, to virtue, to truth, in fact all his important characteristics" (89). Most of what Graves told me about his life was a distraction and void of "important characteristics." So I looked for the greater understanding in the writings of others who had met Graves, especially those who had known him before the myth of the man obscured the personae of the poet.

For the biographer Richard Perceval Graves, nephew of Robert Graves, Graves as poet was fashioned by the entry of Laura Riding, though Graves himself would have been more likely to say as a poet he was fashioned by what occurred in that period of six weeks in 1943 when he wrote the core of *The White Goddess: A historical grammar of poetic myth* (1948). As he said at the beginning of "To Juan at the Winter Solstice," "There is one story and one story only / That will prove worth your telling." That story, of course, is of the White Goddess, the cruel lover of the poet from whom all value descends. In his foreword to *The White Goddess*, Graves explained "the language of poetic myth" as a "magical language" based on the ancient, even Stone Age worship of the Moon Goddess—or the muse. For Graves, such was the "language of true poetry" (6). This goddess fulfilled for Graves all the roles of woman: mother, lover, and layer-out. She also reflected his own experience with woman as demanding, willful, and fickle. As such, she seems a creation by the poet to justify the ways of women to Graves, which is the view of Paul Fussell, who contends that Graves transformed the White Goddess from "psychological metaphor into a virtual anthropological 'fact'" (206). In *The White Goddess,* and frequently before and after, Graves did not distinguish between goddess and muse, placing the power with a woman—often a specific woman. In contradiction to Fussell's view, the goddess came to Graves as an experience and not as an abstraction. There is reason to believe Graves's experience of the White Goddess was real. Graves's daughter, Catherine Dalton, wrote to me on 26 October 1997:

> As for the White Goddess: Father did not conjure up the White Goddess from his mere imagination, but happened to have seen her— just when I have no idea—except that it would have been early in his life. For him to have admitted sighting such an appearance would have gone ill with him, as it would have been judged a serious mental aberration, not an experience shared by other poets (whether ever to be published or not).

That never-before-discussed appearance may well be the seminal experience for Graves the poet. And that he was in the presence of the Goddess at least by 1924 is forcefully evidenced by "A History," a poem called to my attention by Beryl Graves:

The Palmist said: "In your left hand, which shews your inheritance, the Line of Head dips steeply towards Luna. In your right hand, which shews your development, there is a determined effort to escape into less melancholy thinking." I said nothing, but shewed him this sonnet:

> When in my first and loneliest love I saw
> The sun swim down in tears to meet the sea,
> When woods and clouds and mountains massed their awe
> To whelm the house of torment that was me,
> When spirits below the cromlech heard me pass
> Belling their hate with such malignant cries
> That horror and anguish rustled through the grass
> And the very flowers glared up with oafish eyes.
>
> Then round I turned where rose the death-white Fay
> And knew her well that exercised her wand,
> That spurred my heart with rowellings day by day
> To the very reach of madness and beyond,
> Thee, moon, whom now I flout, by thought made bold,
> Naked, my Joseph's garment in thy hold. (CP 3:330–331)

Graves did not choose to reprint this poem, which he published in *Decachord* in 1924, probably for the same reason that his daughter Catherine said he did not speak of having seen the Goddess: he would have been thought mad. Yet he was compelled to publish the poem once. Significantly, he saw the Fay as the power that troubled his life, the trauma of love and war that would be his muse. As in the quotation above from the foreword to *The White Goddess*, Graves frequently does not distinguish between the Goddess and her emissary, the Muse. Most succinctly put: the Muse is the medium through which the Goddess expresses her will. Then, too, Graves believed that the Goddess could express herself directly.

By the forties, when Graves published *The White Goddess*, Jung's concept of the collective unconscious and the archetypes that inhabit it were part of the familiar furniture of our culture. Graves could speak of the White Goddess and be understood, but probably only figuratively, not literally. Yet Jung believed in the actual existence of his archetypes, just as much as Graves believed in the White Goddess. In a letter to Lawrence Durrell dated 15 December 1947 about Durrell's essay recounting his and others' spiritual experiences at sites sacred to Aesculapius, Jung wrote that he had had similar experiences with what he described as "the rather extraordinary relations between our unconscious mind and what one calls time and space." Though Graves was never a Jungian (and eventually rejected his own early interest in depth psychology), he would have understood the experiences of Durrell and Jung. Perhaps we have reduced their experiences to metaphors, using the rhetoric of psychology, to correspond to our secular and literal age. But Graves was not of this age. As John W. Vickery implied, Graves was of that late Victorian time shaken from its unquestioned stability by Frazer's *The Golden Bough*. That study of comparative religions and myths would have lent credibility to Graves for the dream symbols of Freud that were part of his study in the twenties (17–18). Interestingly, Graves was pulled away from the past by the new learning that would shape twentieth-century thought, and pulled back into the past by his own spiritual experiences.

Graves "experienced" the Goddess before he wrote of "the one story" for the first time. And he certainly was an accomplished writer long before he announced her existence. That time and those works are not simply harbingers of his maturity, nor are they simply shapers of it. Those early works are important in themselves, though they also present the elements that form Robert Graves the writer, and surprisingly foretell much about the man. One could say that Graves's neurosis caused him to have hallucinations. He, without a doubt, would say that his neurosis allowed him to see what reason prevented him from seeing. He would throughout his life have experiences or visions induced by drugs or passion, and once in Switzerland, as Beryl told me, from the bite of a snake. Mystics have forever rendered accounts of such visions, and Graves is part of a long and honorable tradition.

In 1925 Virginia Woolf wrote in her diary of finding Robert Graves at her door. By then Virginia and Leonard Woolf had already published Graves at their prestigious Hogarth Press, and he was simply making an unannounced visit to his publishers. He appeared "bolt eyed," hatless, with tousled hair and wearing a blue overcoat, and simply said: "Mrs. Woolf? I'm Graves." Graves stayed longer than she wished, delaying their leaving for the theater to see Shaw's *Caesar and Cleopatra,* and talked of his life. Summarizing the three hours of talk, Virginia Woolf avoided, as was her wont, the niceties of one receptive to a wide range of the human spectrum as she wrote her litany of his improprieties. Graves talked of living outside Oxford with his wife, Nancy Nicholson, who refused the hospitality of Lady Ottoline Morrell; of their four children; of the shop he and Nancy ran; and of his family, including important ancestors whom he despised. She drew the only conclusion she could:

> No I don't think he'll write great poetry, but what will you? The sensitive are needed too, the halfbaked, stammering stuttering, who perhaps improve their own quarter of Oxfordshire. (*Conversations* 7–8)

Yet a year earlier Siegfried Sassoon noted that in a conversation with Virginia Woolf, "We gossiped about the obvious names—Hardy, Gosse, Wells, Lady Colfax, Middleton Murray, T. S. Eliot, Robert Graves, Aldous Huxley etc." (*Diaries* 2:79). No distinction is made here between "Modernist" and "Georgian" or "Edwardian." These are simply poets of significance, of whom Graves was one, a belief that Eliot would reiterate and never renounce. They all shared poetical and historical problems but came to solutions marked by who they were and where they came from. Being placed among the most important of the still-living old and the best of the young was a distinction Graves achieved at the cost of losing his early mentor, Edward Marsh. Marsh did not like or understand *The Feather Bed,* and Graves found himself placating Marsh when he wrote to him from World's End Cottage on 19 December 1921:

> You acknowledge that there is passion & spirit in my new writing; but you can't catch the drift—it isn't, be assured that your brain

is ossifying but that mine is liquefying & *Featherbed* represents a particular variety of liquefaction suited to the problem posed. (BCNYPL)

Although Graves had only four years earlier written to Marsh as "the Father of Modern Poetry" (29 December 1917, BCNYPL), he now found himself explaining his poetic technique. What he termed "associative" and "non-linear" thinking would separate Graves from the Georgians and place him among the writers championed by the Woolfs. Though he would cease to rely on the common sense praised by Marsh, Graves did not become a doctrinaire Modernist. Being English rather than international in life and poetry, Graves developed his poetry from domestic sources, not from those on the continent.

Though Virginia Woolf's reaction to Graves is almost understandable, even predictable, given her adherence to social propriety, how odd that she did not consider the achievement of Graves the poet, who had published *Over the Brazier* (1916), *Fairies and Fusiliers* (1917), *Country Sentiment* (1920), *The Pier-Glass* (1921), and *Whipperginny* (1923). Even odder, she did not seem to value the two volumes of Graves's poetry already published by Hogarth: *The Feather Bed* (1923) and *Mock Beggar Hall* (1924). She, too, must have found the presence of Graves to be a distraction from the person she knew from his writings. In 1925, he would publish two more volumes with Hogarth—one of criticism, *Contemporary Techniques of Poetry,* and one of poetry, *The Marmosite's Miscellany,* in 1926 *Another Future of Poetry* and in 1927 *Impenetrability*, both critical studies.

In 1925, Graves would also publish, with Ernest Benn, his first "collected poems": *Robert Graves*. Graves could no longer be called a "minor" poet. True, he struggled financially to support his growing family and only did so with the assistance of parents and friends. But he had not, at this time, compromised his intention to live by his writing; he would within the year accept a position at the Royal University in Cairo, and resign in less than a year vowing never again to be in anyone's employ. Though not financially independent in 1925, Graves was no innocent in dealing with publishers and agents, as we see in this letter to Eric S. Pinker, who represented Graves (as well as Eliot and Joyce):

I enclose another agreement about a shortish essay for the Hogarth Series. Hogarth Press is the only firm for a book of its kind: I want you to put in your own clause about paying moneys to you; an other [*sic*] reserving Collected Essay rights for a [unreadable] future. (UTHRC)

This letter was written 25 March 1925 from World's End Cottage, Islip, Oxford. The rest of the letter contains equally exacting advice on dealing with "that little eel Martin Secker," who had published *Country Sentiment* and *The Pier-Glass,* and placing various poems and essays, the fictional work *My Head! My Head!* and the projected *Collected Poems.* Graves is certain, specific, and urbane in dealing with his occupation: writer. Careful attention to the conditions of the publication and the terms of the contract characterized Graves. He was not cavalier or incautious with his profession, as he frequently was with people.

Virginia Woolf's depiction of Graves as "halfbaked, stuttering stammering" and not destined to write great poetry is belied by the unavoidable fact of his accomplishments. He was no Siegfried Sassoon, riddled with insecurities and trying to free himself from a futile and meaningless life made possible by an independent income. Yet Woolf's view of him as an idiot savant destined to burn to cinders is understandable. She was nervously fashionable and class-conscious. He could only be charitably classified as outré and bohemian. He would not change, as photographs of him prove: tousled hair, a Spanish hat, and a blue cambric shirt with a red bandana. Perhaps he was, in his own way, as affected as Bloomsbury, just of a style beyond that group; or perhaps he was as unaware as he seemed. The distinction between affected and unaware is, at best, blurred as all of us realize when our own affectations become idiosyncrasies.

Even in his own village of Islip, Graves didn't sit well with the locals, though he presents himself in *Good-Bye To All That* as being accepted as "Captain Graves," who played rugger and sat with the village council. H. E. Palmer wrote of going to visit Graves at Islip in an unpublished essay titled "Robert Graves at World's End" (UTHRC). For him, Graves was a "psychologist, a considerable enigma, and 'Georgian,' a poet who fought in the Great War." A neighbor whom Palmer had asked directions in turn asked Palmer about Graves because they couldn't figure him out and didn't know what he did with his "serious" time. Palmer had gone to see Graves because such poems as "The Dead Fox-Hunter" moved him. This 1915 poem, published in *Over the Brazier,* was written in memory of Captain A. L. Samson and reserves for him in heaven the fox and hounds but does not turn aside from the harshness, and bravery, of his death:

We saw that, dying and in hopeless case,
For others' sake that day
He'd smothered all rebellious groans: in death
His fingers were tight clenched between his teeth (28)

Being reminded of this and similar poems, Graves said that "he wanted to forget it, could not read it with composure." Even then, ten years after the death and seven years after the Armistice, Graves remained intensely troubled by the effects of his wounding, physical and psychological, in the war. This poem was published as part of "La Bassée," the second section of *Over the Brazier.* By then the young man of twenty knew the terms of life in the trenches, yet held closely to his childhood—such as it was. He did not seriously question the privilege and manner of his class, as we see above in his unquestioned approval of fox hunting. He was no Oscar Wilde, waspishly smirking at the "unspeakable chasing the inedible." He never excused the war profiteers; he remained true to his regiment and, without doubt, remained a patriot. He even volunteered for service in World War II but was turned down because of his age. And his pride in and mourning of his son David, who was killed in World War II, were real and unaffected.

Siegfried Sassoon knew Graves better and wrote about him with more awareness and understanding than any of Graves's early friends. Martin Seymour-Smith, commenting on the early days of this friendship, said that when Sassoon had been shocked by Graves's candid and realistic approach to war in his poetry, "Graves told him that when he had been in the trenches he would soon change his style" (42). Graves could not then have predicted how right he was.

As Sassoon admitted, the war ended his "futile" life of hunting and cricket, of quiet and pampered days with the mother who raised him, of petulant quarrels with the executor of his trust when he spent too much on a new horse. Even Cambridge had been too tedious for him to stay more than two years. But where Graves did not fit in the regiment, Sassoon came close. He had the gentlemanly attributes of a sportsman: he looked good in his uniform, he rode well, and he had letters of introduction. He had considerable experience of the world and knew the difference between a good vintage and a mediocre one. In *Sherston's Progress,* the third part of his fictionalized autobiography, *The Memoirs of George Sherston* (1937), he commented that Dr. Rivers, who was treating him for shell shock, "was a good judge of water" (51). Though not as extremely as Graves, Sassoon lived through several different personae in several realities. As Mad Jack he was suicidally heroic; as the acquaintance of Bertrand Russell he was a pacifist willing to risk court martial; as a regular visitor at Garsington he was one of Lady Ottoline Morrell's pets; and then he was the friend and brother officer of Robert Graves.

His first mention of Graves in his diary, he would later extend: "Walked into Bethune for tea with Robert Graves, a young poet, captain in the Third Battalion and very much disliked. An interesting creature, overstrung and self-conscious, a defier of convention" (1:21). A few months later he would describe Graves as "whimsical and queer and human as ever" (1:93). For the next ten years, Sassoon would record meetings with Graves always with a mixture of admiration for his genius and bewilderment because of his idiosyncrasies. In his diary entry for 21 April 1925, Sassoon discusses people in his "personal panorama" who were "essential" to his "mind-life." Robert Graves was essential (2:234). Such a comment indicates Graves's importance, but does not necessarily describe a poet who could be considered one of the "obvious names" in the literary world. Barely thirty at this time, little in Graves's life had prepared him for his genius, much less to be the companion of the great and near-great, the fashionable, and the "obvious." Although he always had, and always would, live among such people, he seemed to protect, to keep in secret, the persona of the poet who drew heart's secrets from the comings and goings in the world around him.

Graves's writings about that war we will look at closely. But a story untold, an underlying text, belongs here, where the central problems lie. As Graves and his biographers have described in detail, his was a nurturing but lonely childhood; he seemed unable to grasp the means of surviving on the school ground. His public school, Charterhouse, never became a place to which he escaped from family, as so often was the case for Victorian and Edwardian young men of the privileged classes. In every way possible, he misunderstood the rules of the community in which he lived. He accepted the relationship encouraged by single-sex schools and had a romance with a younger boy, for Graves an idealistic relationship suitable for a knight and his lady, as this poem, "1915," shows. After describing life in the trenches as the seasons pass from the warmth of spring to a Keatsian "yellowing Autumn" to a winter when he was "knee-deep in mud or snow," Graves professed the love that saved his spirit:

> Dear, you've been everything that I most lack
> In these soul-deadening trenches—pictures, books,
> Music, the quiet of an English wood.
> Beautiful comrade-looks,
> The narrow, bouldered mountain-track,
> The broad, full-bosomed ocean, green and black,
> And Peace, and all that's good.
> (*Over the Brazier* 30)

This Keatsian, and Georgian, poem was written before Graves was told that the object of his devotion, Peter Johnstone, had been arrested for soliciting a soldier. In his preface to *The White Goddess* (1948), Graves would write that "intellectual homosexuality" was "a far more serious moral aberrancy" than actual homosexuality because "it was the male intellect trying to make itself spiritually self-sufficient" (11–12). Graves may well be reflecting on the conventionality of the love that preoccupied him when he was in the army. Not only did he write poems to the young man, but he also asked Edward Marsh about him, indicating the closeness he felt to Marsh. But Graves's comment about the male intellect is far more important than a reflection on an early infatuation. During his first marriage, Graves found that he could not exist as poet simply as a male. As he pursued his poetic gift, he found his androgynous self. As he wrote in "Unicorn and the White Doe," first published in *Whipperginny,* the Doe is "unattainable / Complete, incomprehensible" and prophesies to the Unicorn that there will be "No mate for you" (9–10). Body and Spirit, Unicorn and Doe exist as parts of the eternal search for spiritual meaning: one to seek and the other to be found. The spirit, the feminine, will also appear in more frightful forms.

Graves first published "1915" in "Part I.—Charterhouse," *Over the Brazier* (1916). The other poems echo the young man's loneliness, what in later times would be called "alienation," as in "Cherry-Time" when he recalls a happier time of "fairy piper" and his "magic tune" (16). This jolly little poem is clearly juvenile work, of interest only because it indicates the continued popularity of poetry best written by the young Yeats, because it contrasts so strongly with the poetry in the second section, and because it depicts a life completely different from Graves's life at Charterhouse. Perhaps these cherries were picked in what Graves later called a "secret garden to which you can retreat in your mind" (*Conversations* 57). Even Charterhouse could allow a carefree poem from a young poet significantly separated from his fellows.

Graves avoided continued ragging from the other students by becoming a boxer. His concern with poetry and his unwillingness or inability to fit in made him as "unpopular" at Charterhouse as Sassoon said he was in the regiment. A slight resemblance to Joyce's Stephen Dedalus exists here, but Stephen never drank cherry brandy between boxing matches to fortify himself, nor did he remain "pure" until marriage as did Graves. Graves told me he was pure during the war because he noticed that the men who had women before going into battle were usually killed. He told, perhaps, a partial truth, though he may actually at that time have been so superstitious. In *Good-Bye To All That,* Graves explained his abstinence as caused by a fear of contracting venereal disease, certainly a sensible excuse, though not one to make him better liked by the other officers. Without doubt, he was shy, puritanical to the point of irritation, and probably unwilling to sully the purity of his courtly love for the boy from Charterhouse he called "Dick." A letter to Sassoon, probably in 1916, indicates Graves's high moral tone, as he dismisses his fellow officers because he himself is "unconcerned with smut, sodomy, Sandhurst." Graves was not likely to have kept such views to himself, and whatever the concerns of his fellow officers, such a characterization would antagonize them.

Graves's closest friends at Charterhouse were those who read his poetry, such as the teacher George Mallory, who may have been the first man to reach the summit of Mount Everest. Mallory introduced him to Edward Marsh, progenitor of Georgian poetry, a movement which appears from the vantage of eighty years hindsight to have been hopelessly archaic and anachronistic. But at the time Graves was at Charterhouse, the Georgians were very modern, concerned with resuscitating the dead art of rhyme, as Pound and the Imagists intended as well. Although Graves distinguished between the two by their English and American origins, just as accurately the distinction can be made between poems by those who accepted the importance of the English past, including the rights of the privileged classes, and those who were professional intellectuals, such as Richard Aldington. The differences between Graves and Aldington would later appear very clearly when Aldington published *Lawrence of Arabia: A Biographical Enquiry* (1955). Aldington not only discussed Lawrence's homosexuality, but also questioned the veracity of his representation of his military and political accomplishments. The charge against Aldington was led by Captain Liddell-Hart; both he and Graves had written early biographies of Lawrence at his request. The differences between Aldington and "the Lawrence crowd" were marked by class, with Liddell-Hart and Graves having ready access to No. 10 Downing Street for Churchill's support, and access to publishers to stop Aldington's livelihood. Though Graves decided to let Aldington's biography sink into oblivion, Aldington considered Graves an enemy and the instigator of his problems. However, by then Graves had become a legend unto himself.

What other differences between Graves and the rising professional intellectuals existed do not seem, on Graves's part, to have been ideological. Throughout Graves's life (except for the years with Laura Riding), T. S. Eliot was close, close enough to publish *The White Goddess* at Faber after it had twice been turned down by other publishers. Graves had his own particular view of his efforts at getting the book published, which he discussed in "The White Goddess: A Talk for the Y.M.H.A. Center, New York, February 9, 1957." In this talk he described the effect his manuscript had on the three editors who considered it for publication (WG 504). However, he was much more explicit in telling the tale to his friend Martin Seymour-Smith:

> I sent it to two publishers (OUP and Macmillan). . . . One of these rejected it politely, saying that he would not venture to persuade his colleagues of its merit, though convinced himself. He died three weeks later. Another (American) rejected it impolitely and almost at once was found hanging from a tree in his garden dressed in a skirt, blouse, nylon knickers and a brassiere. I saw the White Goddess's terrible hand in that, but never found what sort of tree it was. Yew? Elder? (Seymour-Smith 398)

After accepting *The White Goddess* for publication, Eliot had a Nobel Prize and an O.M. Reflecting on the history of those who rejected the book and Eliot who accepted it, Graves said to Martin Seymour-Smith: "Makes you think, doesn't it?" (Seymour-Smith 398).

But his view of Pound never changed from the time of their introduction to one another by T. E. Lawrence, which Graves recalled in his 1957 revision of *Good-Bye To All That*: "Ezra Pound: Robert Graves—you will dislike each other" (301). Seymour-Smith recalls a conversation with Graves just after they left Eliot's office. Eliot had asked Graves to sign a petition to have Pound released from St. Elizabeth's, a hospital for the criminally insane, where he had been placed when he was brought back to the United States. Graves declined to sign because he did not value Pound as a poet, the ostensible reason for the petition. Later Graves told Seymour-Smith that he didn't think Pound had "any more literary merit than other traitors" (26). Graves was, as in this discussion with Eliot, always exceedingly honest and, generally, civil. As a poet (and a man of letters), he conducted himself with poise and confidence. Often, though, people with whom he disagreed had cause to consider him "prickly."

Among the poets, if not among the socially self-conscious, Graves moved without restraint and, seemingly, without awkwardness. When at Charterhouse and soon after leaving, he had a young poet's fascination with those who wrote and published—and with those who published them. In a letter written on 3 February 1915, Graves credits Edward Marsh with saving him from the Victorian influences of his father and his uncle. He mentions that in his father's "vinous days," when his inspiration was strong, he had been "hand in glove with Tennyson & Ruskin and that lot & has his memories of Wordsworth" and that with his uncle, C. L. Graves of "The Spectator," had been trying to mold him into that "outworn tradition." Against these influences, he hoped Marsh would provide direction and encouragement (BCNYPL).

Though discrediting the influence of his father and uncle, and flattering Marsh, Graves established his own poetic lineage for his chosen mentor. The letter is a diplomatically accomplished statement by so young a man, indicating how seriously Graves approached his life as poet. But his success would have come more slowly without the continuous efforts made by his father, who spoke with publishers and reviewers.

In this same letter, he credits Marsh with having pulled him into modern poetry:

> However, I am still in my 'teens & when this ridiculous war is over, I will write Chapter II at the top of the new sheet & with the help of other young Georgians to whom I trust you will introduce me, I will try to cut out more effectively the obnoxious survivals of Victorianism. (BCNYPL)

With our hindsight, and his own less than five years after he wrote this letter, he does not seem to have been pulled very far by Edward Marsh. Considering his public school background and his father's considerable literary reputation (a most conservative one), he would naturally respond to the Georgians, who prized so much the England of his father. Even much of his war poetry is informed by the Georgian love of English things, as in "On Finding Myself a Soldier" from *Over the Brazier.* He describes a pretty budding flower with creamy petals:

> But yesterday aghast I found,
> Where last I'd left the bud,
> Twelve flamy petals ringed around
> A heart more red than blood. (18)

As Graves observed, the importance of Georgian poetry at the time was to provide stability, belief in a peaceful past, during the traumatic occurrences of war.

"On Finding Myself a Soldier" does somewhat allay fear, simply by providing a peaceful image. Of great importance is the inability of the peaceful image to endure. It is overcome by the violence. Even "1915," which intends to superimpose the knightly devotion of the lover, fails to sustain the Georgian concern with things English and makes clear the reason: "To winter nights knee-deep in mud or snow, / And you've been everything" (30). The poet holds to the past, but the present is like a deep bruise, constantly and continuously painful. By this time, Graves does not separate love and violence, and an image of one necessitates an image of the other. He exists in a state of incipient anxiety, a prelude to the trauma that will open his mind to the unknown and unseen.

The dreadfulness of the present indicates both the need for the Georgian movement and the certainty of its passing. For those of us who live in a world of machines and their sounds, with the expectations that we (like machines) will act without quirk and without failure, Georgian poetry seems an impossible anachronism. Yet it was not. Georgian poetry expressed a reality that is necessary for us to feel, even vicariously, if we are to understand what formed the experience of the young English gentlemen before their reality became the mechanized hell of the war in France. They knew the quietness of Keats's porcelain lovers, the silence of Coleridge's cottage at night. For them the English past was still alive, and well presented by Rupert Brooke in "The Great Lover":

> White plates and cups, clean-gleaming,
> Ringed with blue lines; and feathery, faery dust;
> Wet roofs, beneath the lamp-light; the strong crust
> Of friendly bread; and many-tasting food;
> Rainbows; and the blue bitter smoke of wood. (121)

Their world disintegrated in the trenches of France and in the politics of the Versailles Conference: the business of twentieth-century culture was upon them. In *A Survey of Modernist Poetry,* Graves wrote of the disillusioned Georgians who retreated from the modern world by Morris dancing into a make-believe one (256). Brooke, in "The Great Lover," wrote of his contemporary world, one he could not imagine ending, one that could even find beauty in "the great machine," not knowing it would destroy him and all he loved. Brooke died on his way to Gallipoli without ever seeing combat. Graves wrote reverently to Marsh about Brooke's death, yet later would be quite disparaging.

Graves would state in 1928 that the trenches made Rupert Brooke "coldly disregarded as indeed he was before his death on active service" (SMP 120). But for those of us not of that time, Brooke's poetry, because it does belong to that fragile idealized past, provides a needed contrast to the real presence of the war as Graves presented it in *Good-Bye To All That*. Describing a bombardment and the effects of a shell bursting overhead, Graves says that his ears "sang" as if there were gnats in them. After the war, he would associate the sound of gnats with his continuing trauma, which he referred to as "war-neurosis" and "neurasthenia." In his first bombardment, the experience of what was doubtless the first of many concussions made his chest "sing," too, and caused him to lose his equilibrium. He was ashamed when the sergeant found him on all fours (112). We should forgive Graves if his memory of such traumatic and youthful experiences is at times faulty, at odds with the facts. Sassoon and Blunden were not forgiving, as indicated by their marginalia in a copy of the 1929 edition of *Good-Bye To All That*. In his edition of the 1929 text, Richard Perceval Graves recorded some of Sassoon's and Blunden's marginal comments (omitting those that were simply vituperative). A representative comment is Sassoon's concerning the presence of lice in the trenches: "None of the dugouts were notably lousy, but R. can't keep the louse out of any war scene" (174). Sassoon had earlier observed that Graves had a nose for whatever was nasty and saw the war as worse than it was. Though Blunden, Sassoon, and Graves would be affected by the war for their entire lives, Graves seems to have had the most deep-seated traumas to deal with.

When Graves revised the 1928 version of *Good-Bye To All That* for the Doubleday edition of 1957, he exorcised the spirit of Laura Riding, just as he had done in the first edition to his first wife Nancy with the urging of Riding. Though the two versions are close, I quote from the first except where Graves's revision includes a reflection missing from the first version.

The continuing effect on Graves of trench warfare was then called "neurasthenia"; we now call it "post-traumatic stress disorder" and have heart-rending experience of many wars as proof of the imprint of battle on the psyche. Although he says he was a friend, not a patient, of W. H. R. Rivers during his period of recovery after the war, Graves subscribed to Rivers's conflict theory: that dreams reflected the unresolved problems of the day. As did Rivers, Graves believed, at this time, that the recurrence of violence and horrors in the dreams of soldiers would disappear as the threat of war declined. The absence of war would dismiss the dreams, and the soldier would be as untroubled as he was before the experience of war. They were wrong. The symptoms may continue for years; indeed, they may continue for most of one's life—as was the case with Graves. The images of violence continued in Graves's writing, informing such seemingly different works as the short story "The Shout" (1929) and the poem "The Cool Web" (1927), the final poem in *Poems (1914–1926)*.

In "The Cool Web," Graves once again wrote a poem about childhood to express his own fears of experiences that were too intense for a sane man. In this poem, images of a war almost ten years past so trouble Graves that he remains unrelieved. Curiously, he links his terror with that of children, as he did frequently in writings about the war. Some recent studies of the symptoms of psychological wounding during war cite close similarities with those of abused children. Graves does not seem to have had such a childhood; and as Catherine Dalton wrote to me on 31 October 1997, hers was a "normal and happy childhood until my parents split up." There is no indication that Graves had discussed these similarities with Rivers, though the two talked often, and Graves repeatedly dealt with the trauma of children.

The pain and horror that even intrude into poems of the "Charterhouse" section of *Over the Brazier* indicate that the tone and narrative of Graves's poems were being interrupted by experiences or memories. Graves gave one possible cause in *A Survey of Modernist Poetry:*

> War-poetry was Georgianism's second-wind, for the contrast between the grinding hardships of trench-service—which as a matter of fact none of the early-Georgians experienced—and the Georgian stock-subjects enumerated above was a ready poetic theme. (120)

Georgian poetry was "to be English yet not aggressively imperialistic; pantheistic rather than aesthetic; as simple as a child's reading book" (119). Though Graves was, in this passage, separating himself from the Georgians, most of his own poems have these qualities. He shared with the Georgians a culture he never completely exorcised. And not even the powerful influence of the young American poet Laura Riding would get him to abandon the uppercase letters at the beginning of a line, or to adopt French or American verse forms. Yet he had changed greatly from the young man who wrote to Edward Marsh on 1 July 1916 asking to be his literary executor. Rejecting his father, Graves declared Marsh to be the only person he could trust and gave him "an absolute free hand" to change or arrange anything he had written (BCNYPL). Not even Brooke had given Marsh such authority, and within five years Graves would not have considered repeating the request.

Even as he continued to write Georgian poems, Graves became skeptical of the commonsense reality that informed Georgian poetry, rooted as it was in the stable prewar society of England's privileged classes, who be-lieved in the Empire they had been educated to serve, believed in unques-tioned patriotism and sacrifice. He acknowledged by 1922 in *On English Poetry* that an "Aristotelian" understanding of reality and art based on the " 'probable and necessary' according to our every-day experiences of life" was no longer tenable for him (72–73). Belief in such a reality had driven Western history, probably, to destroy a generation in the war just ended. Instead of believing in the rational narratives underlying classical tropes, Graves believed that the process of "association," characteristic of the dream state, could lead to a more believable, and more accurate, pre-sentation of the reality of the poet.

Important to this view is Graves's insistence, though only implied, that the presumed objectivity of the past must be abandoned. Reality is not unaffected by our perception because we can only live with what we can see. For instance, Palmer wrote in his essay about visiting Graves that "he seems to be afraid of the moon." Since he was familiar with *Over the Brazier*, he was undoubtedly referring to the poem "I Hate The Moon," included in a section of the book called "Nursery Memories" in the "La Bassée" part of the volume:

> I like the stars, and especially the Big Bear
> And the W star, and one like a diamond ring,
> But I *hate* the Moon and the horrible stony stare,
> And I know one day it'll do me some dreadful thing. (26)

Palmer was clearly puzzled by this portrayal of the moon, so different from the "Jolly Yellow Moon" of the "Charterhouse" section:

> The breath of night blows soft indeed,
> And the jolly yellow moon doth shine. (10)

However, there is no puzzle, just a difference based on experience and situation. Graves in "The Jolly Yellow Moon" had not been in battle. Graves who wrote "I Hate The Moon" very obviously had been in battle, as the comment in parentheses after the title indicates: "(*After a moonlight patrol near the Brickstacks*)," recalling the terror of crawling through no-man's-land brightly lit by the moon. Graves's hatred and terror are under-standable, though their persistence contradicts his "conflict theory." With the ending of hostilities, the moon should have receded into the mist of the past, no longer a bright disk paralyzing a young man's vision. But Graves's awe, or terror, of the moon never abated. Eventually the moon became the sign of the Goddess who was to rule his dreams and his poems. It was a sign of her power as early as 1924 in "A History."

Graves was as unprepared for marriage as he was for war, or so he and his biographers indicate. His wife Nancy Nicholson knew even less and was horrified by giving birth, not having any idea how children were born. Granting such ignorance, we can be just as certain that neither had any idea of the nature of the erotic, though Robert Graves did have some limited experience from his romance with Dick. Undoubtedly, he also knew the fundamentals of sexual congress from the conversations of fellow students at Charterhouse and from those with fellow officers.

With marriage to Nancy, Graves seems to have abandoned his sense of self-determination. She was, by his account, odd for her time and station. She worked as a "land girl" during the war, having chosen to work on a farm rather than go to school, and she changed into her smock and trousers after the wedding ceremony, much to the surprise of Graves's mother. Though Graves and others have cast her as both odd and not very intelligent, her daughter Catherine remembers her very differently, as indicated in her letter to me of 31 October 1997. Her mother took child-rearing seriously and brought her children up with what now would be considered a healthy diet of eggs, vegetables, fruit, homemade bread, porridge, and little meat. At the time her child-rearing was considered eccentric. Also, according to Catherine Dalton, her mother had a fine critical intellect that endeared her not only to her husband but also to Geoffrey Phibbs, with whom she lived after the breakup of the foursome formed by her parents, Laura Riding, and Geoffrey Phibbs during the period Graves referred to as "unpublishable."

Inclined to socialism, Nancy led Robert into opening a shop at the cottage they rented from John Masefield. They sold goods to neighbors, many of whom were working-class, an occupation unusual for people of their privilege. The enterprise failed disastrously, and Nancy decided they should move. As Graves told Virginia Woolf, he found exactly the cottage she described. He did not mention that his mother bought it and then rented it to them. When Sassoon withdrew from Graves's company because of a growing dislike of Nancy, Graves was clear and sharp in delineating the nature of his marriage in a letter dated 31 May [1919] from Islip:

> It boils down to this:—When I married I identified myself & do identify myself more & more with Nancy. If only you had accepted or if only you will still accept us as that physical monstrosity the Phoenix-&-Turtle (see Wm.Sh) the whole conflict finds its solution. You

identify me in your mind as a certain Robert Graves now dead and whose bones & detritus may be found in *Over the Brazier, Fairies and Fusiliers* & the land of memory. Don't. (BCNYPL)

They had four children and lived a bohemian life, never certain of money and always welcome in the homes of the wealthy or for holidays with their parents. Such are the bare bones of their life, one not unfamiliar to parents today or any other day. Yet for Robert Graves, poet, to be lover, husband, and father opened a door into his psyche that was as awe- and terror-inspiring as war.

After *Over the Brazier,* Graves no longer wrote predictable romantic poems. Although *Country Sentiment* (1920) has some "jolly" poems to wife and children, in the context of the volume they are nervously self-conscious, like the whistling of someone passing by a graveyard at night. Poems of the pain of war and of love characterize this volume, dedicated to Nancy Nicholson, as in "Neglectful Edward," a balladesque dialogue between Nancy and her lover:

> "You can keep your pearls and your gold earring,
> And your bird of the East that will not sing,
> But, Ned, have you *nothing* more for me
> Than heathenish gew-gaw toys" says she,
> "Have you nothing better for Nancy?" (67)

The trials of love vied unsuccessfully with the hauntings of war in this volume, but overcame all other concerns in the next two volumes: *The Pier-Glass* (1925) and *Whipperginny* (1923).

Whatever his life was like, the "mind-life" of the poems tells of new hauntings just as terrifying as those of the war. "Reproach," from *The Pier-Glass,* lacks the defined object of the war poems and disturbs both poet and reader by the ambiguity of its source. Responding to a "grieving moonlight face" that reproaches him with the words "unkind, untrue," he can only consider that he is guilty of "ancestral sin"; and he is unable to understand anything else:

> Untrue but how, what broken oath?
> Unkind? I know not even your name.
> Unkind, untrue, you charge me both,
> Scalding my heart with shame. (20)

The poems of childhood so characteristic of Graves's writings in the twenties offer the first refuge for the reader, but the uneasiness here is not that of a child recalling nightmares, so often host to the anxieties of the shell-shocked poet. The certainty of war was replaced by the uncertainty of love; the certainty of violence, by the possibility of betrayal and rejection. But as in other poems Graves wrote at this time, the personage addressed by the poet scarcely achieves individual identity. She is the divinity herself, as yet beyond description for Graves. Even muses such as Nancy never become individual. Goddess or muse, she is the other, a spiritual being, as in "Reproach"—a "moonlight face" that increases, not mitigates, his fear and awareness of personal (though vague) transgression. He would come to see, in time, that his sin was being born into the patriarchy. Only by renouncing it could he delay the fate of the scapegoat. His rejection of his father in *Good-Bye To All That* may well be nothing more sinister than a classic rejection of the father, though Graves would have substituted the eternal feminine for Freud. His later celebration of the Moon Goddess is prefigured in the terror the moon inspires in so many early poems, a terror that would become mixed with awe.

To escape, or at least mitigate, "the emotional intensity" of such poems as "Reproach," in *Whipperginny* Graves evoked legendary beasts such as the White Doe and the Unicorn, and commonplace characters such as John Doe, who cuckolded and so inspired the envy of Richard Roe. These poems, seemingly conventional tales, are more exactly seen as Graves's telling of his fearful muse and of his anxiety lest he lose her: the White Doe of his inspiration in traditional terms, and the John Doe of his personal anxiety. When not casting the tremors of the psyche in symbol or character, Graves's expression of uncertainty is openly painful, as in "A Lover Since Childhood":

> Do but remember, we
> Once could in love agree,
> Swallow your pride, let us be as we used to be. (4)

Understandably, Graves did not reprint this poem in later collections. What little more it does than voice a rather traditional lover's complaint is to portray a Graves who accepts the moods, whims, and decisions of his lover without question. Stunned by the presence of woman, he seemed powerless to do other than accept her beneficence and her punishment. Even at this time, Graves would look in myth and story for narratives and personae to echo and amplify his anxiety. But his immediate source of poems was his personal unconscious, which was quickly being informed by what Jung would call the collective unconscious.

The poems in the "Charterhouse" section of *Over the Brazier* are predictable love poems and escapist poems within the Georgian mode. Many of Graves's poems about the war are equally predictable statements of horror at the carnage, or respect for acts of bravery, or the nature of death, as in "The Leveller," which tells of the death of two soldiers, one young and innocent and the other a grizzled veteran:

> Yet in his death this cut-throat wild
> Groaned "Mother! Mother!" like a child,
> While the poor innocent in man's clothes
> Died cursing God with brutal oaths. (57)

This poem, written when Graves was barely twenty, is representative of his war poems. Though an imitation of Sassoon's, this poem lacks the power of those of Wilfred Owen or even of Siegfried Sassoon. It also lacks the power of the war poems Graves wrote after meeting Dr. W. H. R. Rivers in 1917. While Sassoon was being treated for shell shock by Rivers, the doctor and Graves frequently discussed the origins of dream and poetry. As a direct result of these talks, Graves wrote "The Illogical Element in English Poetry," his B. Litt. thesis at Oxford, which he published as *Poetic Unreason* in 1925. It was preceded by two other studies of poetry and dream that were also the results of talks with Rivers: *On English Poetry* (1922) and *The Meaning of Dreams* (1925).

Essential to Rivers's Freudian-based approach is that dreams, and poetry as well, occur as an attempt to resolve conflict in waking life. He appears to agree with Freud that the dreamer censors the conflict to relieve the anguish that could result from an unrelenting admission and discussion of the experience. So the actual source of the conflict (the latent meaning) is transformed into an acceptable version (the manifest meaning) through the "processes of symbolization and dramatization" (*Conflict and Dream* 19–22). Rivers's influence on Graves is clear in this passage from *The Meaning of Dreams:*

> . . . I have availed myself of the license readily allowed to poets and novelists, that of telling the truth by a condensation and dramatization of their experiences of life—which is, of course, the method of dreams themselves and a good one. (109)

The terms "condensation" and "dramatization" are common terms in psychoanalysis and characterize the approach of both Rivers and Freud, occurring in Freud's *Interpretation of Dreams* to indicate the dreamer's process of using brief "dream-thoughts" to represent "dream-content" (312–313), a process Rivers and Graves referred to as finding the hidden meaning in the latent meaning. The "irrational" process of association rather than the "rational" process sanctioned by Aristotelian thought provided the link between the life of the poet and the poetic act Graves discussed in all three of his early studies. Once again his source was Rivers. However, Rivers largely provided him with the means to understand his own practice as poet; Graves did not simply apply Rivers's theories, though at times he would himself seem to believe he did.

For Rivers, the resolution of the conflict was the purpose of dream and of poem. He does not seem concerned with, or even aware of, a view expressed by a psychiatrist friend of mine, the late Dr. Jean Fanchette. Discussing a longtime patient, a fetishist, Jean was asked how he would cure such a person. He replied that he did not want to cure him; he wanted to make him a "happy fetishist." Graves, too, seems to have been less concerned with eliminating the problem than accommodating it, as he indicated in *Poetic Unreason:* "This book will principally show Poetry as a record of the conflicts between various pairs of Jekyll and Hyde, or as a record of resolution of these conflicts" (52). Even in such an early poem as "1915," discussed above, Graves does not attempt a resolution but records the conflict between his idyllic love and his pain and anxiety in the war. There is much more of Rivers's theories that informs Graves's theories of the poetic act—at this time. But the essential concerns for Graves are clearly the conflict between thought (or the Aristotelian belief in the rational and predictable) and emotion (or the psychoanalytical belief in the irrational and associative); the source of the poem was a present conflict in the poet's life.

During World War I and for at least ten years after the Armistice, as well as during his marriage to Nancy Nicholson and in all future loves, Robert Graves found rational thought no help in guiding, or even coping with, the paradox of his responses: pleasure and pain (even pleasure in pain), fear and anticipation, the extrapolation of our truths from his experiences. Following Rivers's views, Graves asserted that the mind-life of the poet is the origin of the poem; following Rivers again, he believed that early drafts of poems directly express that origin. The real work of the poet, though, is to make his mind-life our personal life or, at least, our public life. Traditionally, classical rhetoric could guide both poet and reader.

Where the reader attempts such an understanding of Graves's writing, the surface will be skimmed. Yet to understand the poem as a reflex of Graves's life through as many as thirty-five drafts would necessitate biographical information so minute and exhaustive that the record would be like a road map identical in size and shape to the road, unrolling endlessly in front of us as we follow it—impossible and undesirable since the map would certainly replace the trip we had been drawn to or forced to make.

So, too, we must remember that Graves has drawn us to him because of what he wrote, not because he had happy or unhappy affairs and marriages, was brave or cowardly. Yet we can never be free of the desire to look beyond the poem into its meaning for the poet. What meaning we discover, if only biographical, may be so simplistic as to denigrate the value of the work itself. Who did what with which and to whom may not tell us much about such a poem, for instance, as "Richard Roe and John Doe," that tale of adultery and envy which Graves wrote long before he and Nancy were drawn into affairs. Granted that the act of reading is often voyeuristic, readers are still left to make sense of why they are drawn to some works. They must also learn why some poems become "the familiar furniture" of the mind, as Graves termed some poems, among them Keats's "Eve of St. Agnes" and Isaac Rosenberg's "Moses." As did Graves, readers of his poems cannot be merely self-serving and solipsistic, but must look for the life and values that drew them, that drew Graves.

As is true for all, Graves wrote autobiographically. But he did not write to delineate the details of his everyday life, even when it was extraordinary and probably "unpublishable." Graves wrote at first of the memories and intuitive responses aroused in him by his traumas: first of war and childhood, then of love. In "poetic unreason" lay his genius. He wrote of (and took his readers to) a greater experience than that of the literal or actual experience. As horrible as the war was for his fellow poets, for Graves it was even worse. He could ease his conscience by writing Sassoon-like attacks on those who profited from the war, and by returning to the war, but he could not escape its effect on his psyche. The war had become entangled with the very fiber of his creativity, intricately bound to all he had ever experienced, because it opened for him a door into his own attraction to violence and power. He would spend his life pulling at the strands of the fabric, and not only when he created battle stratagems in novels such as *I, Claudius* and *The Golden Fleece,* two among many. Of greater importance is his recognition of the role of violence and passion in his spiritual and creative world. He would forever celebrate and annotate this world, bringing us into the dark wood of the Goddess, and into the dark recesses of his spirit and ours. Only when we accept his writings as telling of his spiritual reality directly, not rhetorically, can we approach the awe and terror of Graves's writing. For readers who are able to, Graves's poetry offers the experience of mystical union, with all its awe and terror. For others, his poetry tells of one man surviving the traumas of war and sexual passion.

CHAPTER 2

THE LUNATIC

War

(Nursery Memories)
III.—I HATE THE MOON

(After a moonlight patrol near the Brickstacks)
I hate the Moon, though it makes most people glad
    And they giggle and talk of silvery beams—you know
But she says the look of the Moon drives people mad,
    And that's the thing that always frightens me so.

I hate it worst when it's cruel and round and bright,
    And you can't make out the marks on its stupid face,
Except when you shut your eyelashes, and all night
    The sky looks green, and the world's a horrible place.

I like the stars, and especially the Big Bear
    And the W star, and one like a diamond ring,
But I *hate* the Moon and its horrible stony stare,
    And I know one day it'll do me some dreadful thing.

Fairies and Fusiliers

When I went to Deya de Mallorca in 1969 to visit Robert Graves, I stayed in a small pension run by his son William. I asked William if I should telephone his father before going to see him. William laughed and said, "You'll have to go see him because Robert doesn't have a telephone." Graves had been shocked by a telephone when he was in the trenches in France during World War I and still smarted from it "until some twelve years later" (GBTAT 107). As is true in general, Graves understated the permanent change to his personality and life brought on by shell shock. He would never completely recover, never again be the innocent he was before the war. Nor would his society: all was changed.

    Quite likely Graves's aversions for the telephone and for trains were also signs of the complex trauma of the war, a war of unprecedented horror: a mechanized hell. When Graves joined the British army in 1915, he and the rest of England expected a short conflict with the heroics and human error of war in the nineteenth century. Most people expected, at the very worst, a repetition of the failed attack Tennyson celebrated in "The Charge of the Light Brigade," a poem once known by every school child:

'Forward the Light Brigade!'
Was there a man dismay'd?
Not tho' the soldier knew
Some one had blunder'd.
Theirs not to make reply,
Theirs not to reason why,
Theirs but to do and die.
Into the valley of Death
Rode the six hundred. (52)

A boy of nineteen certainly could not foresee that every characteristic Tennyson commemorated would die in the trenches of France, every one except the blunders. Graves and his comrades would be dismayed, some to the point of breakdowns and some to the point of self-inflicted wounds. A "blighty," a disabling but not serious wound, could get a man home—at least for a while. That soldier and his comrades would reason why and make reply. Siegfried Sassoon did reason why in an open letter voicing pacifist views in *The Times,* for which he would have been court-martialed if Graves had not intervened. Some, including Sassoon, Graves, and Owen, would reason why in poetry that condemned the war and the waste of lives yet never denied the heroism of their comrades. Graves would never lose his loyalty to his comrades and to his regiment, the Royal Welch Fusiliers; yet he was always quick to condemn those who made a profit from the war. For example, in the children's story *An Ancient Castle* (written during the 1930s), Sergeant George Harington, keeper of Lambuck Castle, a historic ruin, recalls the poor-quality jam sold to the army by Anderson Wigg, knighted for his effort. Whether the strategies and tactics of battle were a passion or an inescapable obsession, Graves returned to them continually in his fiction. His historical novels of the thirties and forties reveal a serious concern with battle, whether in the Roman times of Claudius or the heroic days of Hercules. It was, in fact, while studying admiralty maps as he wrote *The Golden Fleece* that he began to write what would become *The White Goddess.*

The war stayed with Graves in more than anecdote and a lifelong fascination with the management of war and the placement of troops. The

Robert Graves, 1914, in the uniform of a lieutenant of the Royal Welch Fusiliers

war inflicted severe injury on both his body and mind, and destroyed the idealism he had acquired as a young officer in the Royal Welch Fusiliers. The regiment had a long and honorable history, but its officers and soldiers were more familiar with the battles of the nineteenth century than the perils of the twentieth. But they all soon learned better, as Graves implies in describing their arrival in Bethune. The artillery fired a few yards from them, and German shells exploded close. Even so, the war was not yet as bad as it would get with the introduction of "Lewis or Stokes guns, steel helmets, telescopic rifle-sights, gas-shells, pill-boxes, tanks, trench-raids, or any of the later improvements in trench-warfare" (GBTAT 94).

Though Graves experienced danger and discomfort during his first trench duty at Cambrin in 1915, he recalled that as being "lucky" compared to what was soon to come. His poem "1915" reflects his own innocence and also the influences of the Romantics and the Georgians. For reasons of class and time, Graves was much influenced by the poetry of Rupert Brooke and others championed by Edward Marsh, a poetry of "little England" with its public schools and privileged classes, with its images of the English countryside, the playing field, tea served in Wedgwood china. The inheritors of the cultural and political power of England, the Georgians were not likely to share the efforts of Pound and the Imagists/Vorticists to throw out both bath water and baby by replacing cultural context with an isolated image, as Pound did when he reduced "In a Station of the Metro" from thirty lines to a mere two. We must remember that some of the poems in *Over the Brazier* were written in the Everyman edition of Keats's poetry given to Graves by his father. In *Good-Bye To All That,* he also wrote of the cold and wet clothing, the mud, yet he avowed the courtly approach to war and love, which also characterizes this poem, written for his Charterhouse love, the boy he referred to as Dick. Openly discussed in *Good-Bye To All That,* the love seems the most innocuous kind that develops in single-sex schools. In any case, Graves contended that it was not erotic, and his innocence at the time of his marriage would lend credence to his claim. Throughout life, he was romantic and courtly in his poetry, unusually so for a man whose life was at times scandalous.

The story of Graves's life with Laura Riding has been told often by his biographers and alluded to by Graves himself in "Dedicatory Epistle" to the 1928 edition of *Good-Bye To All That:*

How, though you knew no more of us than we of you, and indeed less (for you knew me at a disadvantage, by my poems of the war), you forthwith came. And how there was thereupon a unity to which you and I pledged our faith and she her pleasure. (322)

The implied judgment of Nancy as concerned only with her pleasure seems revisionist, at least in terms of Graves's comments at the time they were all together. As he wrote to Sassoon, he was unconcerned with any scandal and pleased with the arrangement:

> She [Nancy] has longed for this privacy for years to start her drawing again and regain some sort of independent completeness, & now there's a nurse for the children & Laura to look after me, it is too good a chance to miss. But I see you shaking your head! Sighing! (BCNYPL)

The story is a complex one of passion and jealousy, of danger and violence, that did not directly become part of Graves's poetry. Many years later, when he was in his sixties, Graves began a series of affairs with young women known as his muses. The poetry written to them is often explicit, yet always romantic and courtly, frequently with a naiveté reminiscent of the poems of his youth. Most certainly if we consider the innocence with which he approached love in 1915, Graves was no more prepared for the erotic than he was for trench warfare. And in his mind, the two became linked.

Of more importance in "1915" than the admission of his relationship with Dick is Graves's portrayal of his life in England, one with books and art, with love and quiet. Repeatedly in *Good-Bye To All That,* Graves recalls the noise of battle, which must have been mind-jarring especially for someone such as Graves who had spent so much of his life in rural England and Wales. Even during his "lucky" assignment, he noted the noise. In a letter in 1915, Graves describes a colossal bombardment by the French at Souchez, a few miles from him, that is so loud as to seem palpable to feeling as well as to hearing, causing him to observe that "the whole air rocked and shook." The next day he heard that a thunderstorm had occurred during the bombardment, leading one of the soldiers to observe that where "the gunder ended and the thunder began was hard to say" (105). He wrote to Edward Marsh three months earlier, on 15 March 1915, that sound was palpable in battle:

> I have to get used to all the old noises, from the crack crackity-ockity-ockity-ockity-ockity, ockity, ockity of a rifle bullet to the boom! . . . swish . . . swish. GRR, GRR GRR ROAR! Of a fifteen inch shell. (BCNYPL)

Other letters from Graves include simulated sounds of battle, which became an indelible part of his perception of war and trauma. Though the poems in *Over the Brazier* were written before Graves had been shell-shocked, wounded, or had a breakdown, they clearly present the war that had substituted itself for his past reality. In the titular poem of *Over the Brazier,* Graves tells of men talking around the charcoal brazier on an April night near La Bassée of idyllic lives in Canada or the South Seas. He knew these were empty dreams, as empty as his own dream of a cottage in North Wales with books and a garden where he would "dream and write" (31). Even so early in the war, Graves was aware that such a dream was like whistling in the dark, evoking the peaceful to ward off the presence of death. His poems about night patrol and corpses lack the force and detail of this simple scene from the life of a man who had lived with privilege and always would.

Quite likely, Graves the poet could not accommodate as much of the force of the war as could Graves the writer of fiction. In fiction and nonfiction, Graves wrote on a variety of subjects: the myths of Greece, Rome, and Christianity; the wars of ancient and modern times; the nature of poetry and religion. Poetry would be his vocation, and prose a profitable avocation. And he would remain steadfastly in his own version of the English tradition. Never would Graves the poet abandon the English countryside, not even when he took up residence in Mallorca in 1929. And the spiritual world would always be the central concern of his poetry, though he could write occasional poems.

In *Good-Bye To All That,* when writing about the time before the Somme offensive, Graves observed that aside from "wounds, gas, and the accidents of war," the soldiers' lot was not unhealthy. The plentiful food and work in the open air made up for such discomforts as wet feet and drafty quarters (158). However, when writing about his particular situation, Graves was much less sanguine when he described what he and his fellow officers knowingly faced during the war. He described his understanding when he had been in the trenches for five months and was getting past his prime. An officer needed three weeks to learn his way about and was at his best for the next four months unless he suffered severe shock—or a series of shocks. Inevitably, neurasthenia developed after four months. With time in a rest camp or hospital, he could be reasonably effective up to ten months. After a year, he was "worse than useless." Officers were twice as likely as the men to be wounded or killed, or to suffer neurasthenia. Graves considered himself too young to be there since the optimum age for an officer was between twenty-three and thirty-three. That officers were both younger and older than the optimum is a startling demographic

(GBTAT 157–159). A large part of the appeal, and value, of *Good-Bye To All That* rests in Graves's explaining the experiences of those who fought in World War 1 to those who did not. Yet on reflection, his readers must realize the difference between their understandings and Graves's. In this passage Graves discussed the inevitability of neurasthenia, or death, with a matter-of-factness unthinkable for civilians. Graves's memoirs are quite readable, written (as was much of poetry about war) for those who shared his experiences and with the understanding that he was different from those who had not shared his experiences. "Limbo," in *Over the Brazier,* not only describes the soldier's life but also, as significantly, the difference between his reality and that of those not part of the battle. After a week of rain and death, of the "roars and whirrs and rattles" of battle, there was a respite into the unreality of a peaceful farmland of horses, crops and babies (22). Recognizing the very modest poetic value of "Limbo," Graves did not reprint it. But the poem does indicate the nature of his talent. He was not one of those made a poet by war, which he observed was true for many. I remember reading poems by a friend when he was fighting in Vietnam; now a general officer, he is no longer a poet. But Graves, even during World War I, was never a war poet, but a poet who wrote about war. He was right in not valuing highly his war poems. Their value is in revealing the effect of battle on Graves's creativity. Though he never completely abandoned the life of privileged classes in England as much as is implied by the title *Good-Bye To All That,* that book and his poems written during and about the war indicate his separation from what he had earlier accepted as reality.

The innocence of the poems in *Over the Brazier* was lost when Graves took part in the Battle of the Somme, which marked him for life. Nothing Graves or any other soldier—German, French, or English—had experienced could have prepared them for this battle in which the commanders' blunders and the huge loss of life made the destruction of the Light Brigade seem paltry. John Keegan, in *The Face of Battle,* describes the seven-day bombardment by the British that preceded the Battle of the Somme. The British fired "about 1,500,000 shells," most of which were "18-pounder shrapnel shells" (231). Despite the obvious trauma of constant shelling, the British bombardment did not destroy the entrenched German machine guns. So as they advanced during the planned lulls in bombardment on the first of July, the British soldiers were slaughtered. The battle continued with renewed attacks until 18 November 1916, at which time the British casualties numbered 419,654 and those of the French 200,000 (the German number was undetermined) (Kegan 280). The battle line stretched over fifteen miles, most of which was torn up to a depth of six feet. Of the memoirs of the battle, Graves's is representative, though re-strained even when recalling when he was wounded during a bombard-ment of "heavy stuff," six- and eight-inch guns. As he figured out when he examined his wounds later, an eight-inch shell had exploded close behind him as he ran. The shock of the shell was like a punch in the back that numbed him, and he did not realize he had been hit until blood ran into his eye. After calling out that he had been hit, he felt faint and fell down (GBTAT 195). When the dead at the aid station were being cleared away, someone noticed that Graves was breathing. His parents had been notified of his death by a letter dated 16 July and would not learn until the 24th that their son was alive. He had a bad time of it: he was left lying on a stretcher with his bandages unchanged for five days for fear of restarting the bleeding. He described the trip by train to Rouen as "nightmarish" (262–268). Although his fear of train rides would not abate for many years, Laura Riding was able to convince him to travel to Sligo, then Rouen, and finally to Huntington by a private train to retrieve Geoffrey Phibbs from his wife. Phibbs had made the threesome a foursome and would later choose to live with Nancy Nicholson rather than Laura Rid-ing, prompting the latter to step out of a fourth-story window with a "Goodbye, chaps" (Seymour-Smith 166).

Graves and Sassoon rejoined the Second Battalion at Litherhead near Liverpool in November of 1916. Within a month of non-combat activity, Graves "was glad to be sent up to the trenches" (GBTAT 215). Back at the Somme, however, his health declined; and he was sent back to England, to Oxford as he requested. Graves published his poems about the Somme in *Goliath and David* in an edition of about two hundred copies which were not for sale. Fred Higginson observed that this volume may actually have been published before *Over the Brazier,* which Graves named as his first volume (8–9). Publishing history aside, the poems in *Goliath and David* deal with a later time than those in *Over the Brazier* and move Graves even closer to his breakdown. He notes this difference in "The Dead Boche," which he addressed to those who had read his "songs of war" and only heard of "blood and fame." He offers a "certain cure for lust of blood" in telling of what he found in Mametz Wood:

> In a great mess of things unclean,
> Sat a dead Boche; he scowled and stunk
>   With clothes and face a sodden green,
>   Big-bellied, spectacled, crop-haired,
> Dribbling black blood from nose and beard. (30)

In *Good-Bye To All That,* Graves recalled what occasioned this poem, an excursion into Mametz Wood to gather German greatcoats to use as blankets. Every tree in the wood was broken, and he found only one route through the litter of trees and limbs. That route led past a bloated and stinking German corpse that had been there for days. Graves simply observed: "There had been bayonet fighting in the wood" (189). Though closely similar, the two descriptions of the dead German soldier differ in that the prose version provides context which shows the enormity of the destruction. Of course, poetry as a genre is more concerned with the immediate sensation than is nonfiction prose. But in this, and most of his war poems, Graves's poetry was less forceful and less effective than his prose in expressing his increasing horror as his neurasthenia developed. Perhaps only in recollection could Graves write powerfully of such experiences. Later Graves would revise poems as many as thirty-five times, with ten revisions being common. But in the war poems, he revised less if at all. When effective, the poems relied on a context other than the war.

Graves's use of analogy to write about the violence of battle is, according to Elaine Scarry in *The Body in Pain,* also evident in writers from Homer to the present:

> Every temptation to invoke analogies to remote cosmologies (and there is a long tradition of such analogies) is itself a sign of pain's triumph, for it achieves its aversiveness in part by bringing about, even within the radius of several feet, the absolute split between one's sense of one's own reality and the reality of other persons. (4)

Considering that Graves wrote his first poems as analogies in the edition of Keats given to him by his father, we may assume he did so without the luxury of other paper—probably during a lull in the battle. Thus, Professor Scarry's implication that the use of analogy is necessary, and perhaps unconscious, does much to explain these poems by Graves. He was not writing analogies to explain himself to readers lacking his experience. Instead, he was finding images and narratives in the remote cosmology of his childhood—when violence seemed to make sense or at least had been survived.

Poems from this period that I have seen in manuscript are the poems gathered in *Over the Brazier* in the section titled "Nursery Memories" which were taken directly from the pages of the Everyman edition of Keats in which Graves had written them in 1915. In the three poems, after the title Graves wrote a parenthetical comment that indicated the circumstance he chose to present analogously as a tale recollected from childhood rather than as a re-creation of his experiences in battle. Titles and parenthetical comments are:

I.—THE FIRST FUNERAL
(The first corpse I saw was on the German wires, and couldn't be buried)

II.—THE ADVENTURE
(Suggested by the claim of a machine-gun team to have annihilated an enemy wire party: no bodies were found however)

III.—I HATE THE MOON
(After a moonlight patrol near the Brickstacks)

Of these three, "The First Funeral" most movingly presents the analogy. Graves, again, separates his experiences in the trenches from what civilians know, but he holds to a reality from peacetime. Although the parameters of decency changed for him during the war, he was unwilling or unable to abandon the sensibilities that defined his life before he became a soldier. Yet his life in battle was unlike anything he had ever experienced and would make him see all aspects of life, especially friendship and love, in unprecedented ways. Like Sassoon, Graves frequently felt guilty for being alive while so many comrades were dead. When out of action, they felt compelled to return yet were repulsed by the waste of life and fearful for their own lives. The war opened a door into horror for Graves. When he went through it, he often found himself in the nursery and, later, in the marriage bed. In his life, probably only the nightmares and dreams of childhood were at all similar to the nightmarish reality of war. All values and relationships were utterly changed for him by the war, though for some time he only had the language and experiences of peacetime to express this new horrible reality.

In "Goliath and David," first published in a volume of the same title, Graves continued the technique of "Nursery Memories": an italicized comment followed by an analogously related poem: *"(For Lieut. David Thomas, 1st Batt. Royal Welch Fusiliers, killed at Fricourt, March 1916)."* What follows is a jaundiced retelling of the biblical story, ending with the death of David, not of Goliath:

One cruel backhand sabre-cut—
I'm hit! I'm killed! young David cries,
Throws blindly forward, chooses . . . and dies.

Steel-helmeted and gray and grim
Goliath straddles over him. (6)

Graves's traditional Christianity was another casualty of the war. And the reversal of fortunes in this poem indicates this change, signified, as so much of Graves's trauma was, by sound: the loud laugh of the "Steel-helmeted and gray" Goliath who can "scatter chariots," much as he would shells. Such a warrior would have been seen often by Graves as he looked at the Germans across no-man's-land and up close. And young David's cries would have been all too familiar for Graves, both from what he heard and what he himself exclaimed when wounded at the Somme.

Of growing concern for Graves, and Sassoon, would be the lack of understanding the people at home in England had of the war. The soldiers' sense of being pawns and victims would increase their sense of isolation and, ironically, make them long to return to battle. In a "facetious marginal note" to "Goliath and David," Graves made clear his disillusion with the people back in England, whom he held responsible for continuing the war. He imagined a war fought by the Jesses not the Davids, one in which the young send the old to battle and put a card in the window as the "lucky old men" go off to the front singing "Tipperary" (GBTAT 206).

At this point in the war, Graves did not express hatred of the Germans, nor did he understand it, as is clear from his depiction of a bayonet drill at Rouen just before he returned to the Somme. According to *Infantry Training, 1914,* the soldier's purpose is to render the enemy ineffective. The revision of this statement taught the troops that their duty was to hate the Germans and kill as many as possible, to hurt the enemy, to tear out their "guts," to unman them: "WORRY HIM AND EAT HIS HEART OUT." Graves was glad to return to the front (GBTAT 211). Neither he nor Sassoon had any desire to kill the enemy when they returned. They intended to protect and do their best for the men they commanded, though if duty demanded, they would kill Germans. They felt neither the patriotism nor the hatred of non-combatants. Instead, they were bonded with others in a struggle now deprived of any meaning except survival. Duty and bravery were to their comrades, the regiment, but not to England, a land so removed from them that it was an abstraction understood only by memories of peacetime. Then they and those who would not go to war had shared the same reality.

Graves's ambivalence about battle was also reflected through memories of childhood. Frequently as analogues of battle, these memories were treated with irony. The experiences of childhood acquired a newfound respect; and he wrote in "Babylon" of losing touch with the true poet, the child. Gone are Jack the Giant-killer, Oberon, Robin, and Red Riding Hood. Of all "the magic hosts" only a few of "timorous heart" remain, "weeping for Babylon" (GD 9). Steadily Graves is, probably consciously, substituting his experiences and stories for the ideas about childhood so endemic to the English tradition. He does not, however, go so far as to replace Stevenson's *Child's Garden of Verses* with a *Child's Charnel House of Verses*. He was too much a product of his culture (and too much of a Georgian) to do that. Also, he needed a dream to hold on to, what he would much later call a "Secret Garden," a private place. This garden appeared often in Graves's poems, without doubt as early as *Goliath and David*. In "The Bough of Nonsense," the first poem in the volume, two fusiliers "limped painfully home," aged and worn beyond their years. The two, simply called "R." and "S." (clearly Robert and Siegfried), reflect on the changeless fact of nature and the fragile ideologies of humans. They are caught between the two in an uneasy and haunted life, as the last stanza indicates:

> *I tell him of Galatian tales:*
> *He caps them in quick Portuguese,*
> *While phantom creatures with green scales*
> *Scramble and roll among the trees.* (3)

This secret, imagined garden is their only retreat from war, though they clearly longed for the quiet and peaceful gardens they had actually known rather than the exotic melange of this one.

Although his English childhood lost its simple wonder in the trenches of France, Graves steered by the English countryside of the Romantics and Georgians as a fixed point in a constantly changing and eroding reality. In the last poem in *Goliath and David,* "Not Dead," Graves reflects on the loss of his friend David Thomas, whose death he had commemorated a few pages before in "Goliath and David." We must wonder to what extent Graves was able to distinguish the dream world of the poem from the world of war:

> I laugh at chaffinch and primroses.
> All that is simple, happy, strong, he is.
> Over the whole wood in a little while
> Breaks his slow smile. (17)

Mametz Wood at the Somme was a place of death and terror, so Graves replaced it with the comfortable and familiar English wood of his boyhood. Later he would merge the two into a wood of danger and passion, terror and peace, much as Keats did in "La Belle Dame Sans Merci," a poem Graves would discuss in detail in his first critical study of poetry, *On English Poetry*. After the war (though after his marriage is a more likely starting point), Graves's dreams would be inhabited by women, succubi, who came in the quiet of night in the seclusion of the country, leaving him when he awoke as distracted as Keats's knight, who had also been visited by a succubus:

> And this is why I sojourn here,
>   Alone and palely loitering;
> Though the sedge is withered from the Lake
>   And no birds sing.

As Graves indicated in *On English Poetry*, "La Belle Dame Sans Merci" had particular relevance for him in its linking of love and death—a relevance Graves as a youthful reader of Keats had yet to discover, but which was a fixed point for Graves the married veteran. Graves considered that Keats's passion for Fanny Brawne, an unrequited one, conflicted with Keats's own "apprehension, not yet a certainty, of his own destined death from consumption." Thus the lady without mercy represents "both the woman he loved and the death he feared, the woman whom he wanted to glorify by his poetry and the death that would cut his poetry short" (51–52). As Graves said in his discussion, he intended to demystify the poem and wrote for "those braver minds who can read 'The Golden Bough' from cover to cover and still faithfully, with no dawning contempt, do reverence to the gods of their youth" (54–55). Graves came close to saying that for Keats, the Lady was reality experienced, not a metaphor. For readers of Graves, there is an even stronger shock in realizing that he probably experienced the reality of the fearful and awful succubi in his poems. However, he had not yet been deprived of his confidence in the patterns of science, in this case psychoanalysis and its comfortable answers. The inexplicable creatures of the imagination were the workings out of the problems of the day.

But in 1916, Graves awake lived a nightmare; asleep he had a retreat to the peaceful past, a past he still thought might be recoverable. It would be, in poetry, but only in flashes and never as simply as he presented it in "Not Dead." The war opened a door into the unconscious, as he would later discover in discussions with the psychologist W. H. R. Rivers, who treated Siegfried Sassoon and hundreds of other soldiers. As Rivers observed, World War I brought into being the modern practice of psychiatry. The surgical techniques had been developed through the wars of the nineteenth century, but never before had there been so many emotionally wounded as when the young men came back from France. Graves's own wounding imprinted his life forever.

In *Good-Bye To All That*, Graves gave the specifics of his wounding and treatment as well as the accompanying disorientation and emotional instability, including petulance and nervousness. Yet in the poem "Escape" (GD) Graves revealed the psychological (or religious) consequences of his wounding. The last republication of "Escape" was in *Poems (1914– 1927)*. Though Graves was right in eliminating the poem from his oeuvre, it deserves attention here because of what it reveals about Graves the poet during the most critical point of his youth. In keeping with his practice, Graves began with a historical comment: "*(August 6th, 1916.—Officer previously reported died of wounds, now reported wounded. Graves, Captain R. Royal Welch Fusiliers)*." The poem which follows tells of his awakening from a morphine-inspired dream after he had been left for dead. He cheated death by using "the all-powerful poppy" to drug Cerberus and escape back to life (15–16). The poem adds little to the story of Graves's escape from death—except for the sounds he associates with the trauma: his "poor buzzing head" and the roaring and clattering of the demons, heroes, and policemen who chased after him. The roaring and clattering can easily be identified as the sounds of battle, the firing of guns and the movement of troops. The buzzing is altogether different, as it describes Graves's inner world rather than the world outside him. The result of a concussion (or repeated ones), this buzzing noise would reappear as a sound associated with "shell shock" in "The Gnat," which he published in *The Pier-Glass* (1921) and discussed as a war poem in *The Meaning of Dreams* (1924).

Though clearly angered by the harm done to his mind and body, Graves in "Escape" clings to what he has: army-issue jam and morphine. As Cerberus is satiated by them, so is Graves. The jam recalls earlier pleasant days, and the morphine dulls the present pain. Graves does not, at this time, abandon the life and culture that did him such harm. As he would do in all his writings, he would make the daily parts of his life into signs of its value, of his desires. As such, images become symbols, yet images still of a life he needed and loved. Yet that life existed only momentarily in fact, finding its fixed reality in his poetry.

The structure and technique of "Escape" tell much about Graves's state of mind at the time. He continued to use an italicized comment to indicate the particular event that occasioned the poem and, then, wrote a poem analogously related to the event. Graves was a young poet without the skills he would soon develop, so he understandably repeated what had been successful for him. Of more importance, though, is his attempt to impose the language and experience of his present reality as a soldier on Greek myth. He would continue to use and study the myths of Greece and Rome throughout his life, as he would Jewish and Christian texts, usually with the intent of correcting what he regarded as error, much as he did in "Goliath and David" when he reversed the outcome. Graves had the classical education of his class; but he never accepted its confines, though he would never completely leave it. Excepting the controlling influence of women, Graves always seems to have made up his own mind. At least he gives that impression in his writings, the most significant of which, obviously, he wrote after he joined the army at the age of nineteen. His juvenalia did not foreshadow his later writings.

As generally happens, the war separated Graves from his past, as in the language of "Escape." In his mature poetry, Graves avoided jargon or even contemporary usage; "Escape" uses both. The words "Webley," "bombs," "Tickler's jam," and "leave" were common to soldiers but not part of common usage and certainly not part of the language he would later use when he decided to escape from the limitations of time. Indeed, he even changed "Tickler's" to "ration" when he revised the poem for publication in *Poems (1914–1926)* (59). Even in the clause "The crowd swarms on" he is quite likely using "crowd" in the way his comrades did. The colonel who had written to Graves's mother wrote to Graves after hearing he had survived to say how pleased he was to hear that Graves lived. Then, one soldier to another, he told Graves of the "rotten time" they had in the battle, suffering heavy losses largely because of "that rotten crowd" they had collected (59). Sassoon distributed 118 of the 200 copies of the privately printed edition of *Goliath and David* as Graves directed him. Clearly, this volume was meant to be read by Graves's fellow officers, men who shared his education as well as the experience of the army (Higginson 8–9). Graves assumes understanding of his references: Cerberus as the three-headed dog that guards the gate of the Underworld, Lethe as the river one crosses over into the Underworld, and Proserpine as the goddess forced to spend part of each year in the Underworld as the wife of Hades, returning to the upper world in Henna, where Hades first saw her.

The use of classical myth in a contemporary context is similar to what

Auden would later do in "The Shield of Achilles" or to what Eliot would do repeatedly, though most notably in *The Waste Land.* Indeed, Graves would soon be mentioned with Eliot, especially since they considered writing a book together on modernist poetry (Eliot's part was preempted by Laura Riding). Such a link with Eliot indicates not only Graves's prominence but also the shared poetic, if not personal, experience of these two young modern poets. Both found themselves accounting as best they could for the dissociation between past and present that culminated in the violence and politics of World War I. Their best resulted in unforgettable poems.

After the Somme, Graves regarded the war as simply an engagement between trade rivals, one that was continued for profit. Yet he remained an officer who respected his regiment and cared deeply for his comrades. The regiment sustained him as Nancy did later, giving meaning to life and death. Still, his continuing ambivalence is clearly reflected by his concerns in *Fairies and Fusiliers,* his next book of poems. As he explained in *Good-Bye To All That,* he and Sassoon contrasted the war with their "definitions" of peace. Sassoon was concerned with hunting, the countryside, and music. Graves was mainly concerned with children; and when he was in France, he spent much of his spare time playing with them in the villages where he was billeted. He put those children and memories of his own childhood at Harlech into *Fairies and Fusiliers,* which he dedicated to the regiment (206).

The effort to escape war through poetry was not, however, completely successful. Since he was in battle or suffering from its effects, he was ambivalent. In "The Spoilsport" Graves gives ambivalence a ghostlike form. Ghosts, it seems, were as commonplace in France as in Shakespeare's plays and probably for the same reasons, to give expression to the unutterable:

> My familiar ghost again
>   Comes to see what he can see,
> Critic, son of Conscious Brain,
>   Spying on our privacy. (FF 47)

Graves's hauntings in this poem emphasize the rapidly diminishing value of Aristotelian thought, sweet reason being a stranger to the war. Such thinking was unable to answer his problems or exorcise his ghosts. Though he would like to mount a conscious retreat to the memories of childhood, he seldom could without the intrusion of his nightmarish waking life. Even memories of childhood's games turn bitter and provide material for "The Next War." Graves cautions the young that as they play with toy weapons in their father's hayloft and play at being Royal Welch Fusiliers, they are in fact preparing

> To serve your Army and your King,
> Prepared to starve and sweat and die
> Under some fierce foreign sky,
> If only to keep safe those joys
> That belong to British boys. . . . (63–64)

Graves does not simply describe the war by contrasting it with children during peace but suggests that the will to battle may be intrinsic to the species. Yet the passion of the poem is aroused by the threat to British boys, fighting once again to protect the homeland from invasion. Graves and so many young men since him have gone readily to war believing that they were all standing between the enemy and the safety of the home. Graves's experiences in war deprived him of this idealism. The irony of this poem is an important expression of Graves's attitude at the time. He wrote to Sassoon on 13 September 1917 from Litherland, a debarkation port for France, that his decision to dedicate *Fairies and Fusiliers* to the regiment was not only to avoid slighting friends and family but also to "strengthen my expression of hatred for the War." As he indicates in the rest of the poem, war has cunning and cruelty, nastiness and foul tricks, pomp, greed, and rage; yet too there is glory.

Graves does not associate his own envisioned death with glory. Instead, his death seems to him an acting out of the terror of childhood. So powerful is his memory in "A Child's Nightmare" that even his controlling use of analogy does not provide comfort; the traumas of death and childhood are inseparable, as shown in this poem Graves published in *Fairies and Fusiliers* but chose not to reprint. In it Graves tells of being wounded through the memory of a childhood dream of a cat, a dream that came to him in the morphine-induced nightmare that followed his wounding. Graves associated the reappearance of the dream with the train ride he had described as "nightmarish," explaining his lifelong dread of train rides. The cat

> Overpowered me foot and head,
> Lapped my blood, while on and on
> The old voice cruel and flat
> Says for ever, "Cat! . . . Cat! . . . Cat! . . ." (74)

But the nightmare in this poem is not of a cat that will lap his blood, but of a cruel, threatening, and abusive figure. In *Poetic Unreason,* Graves provided a source for the poem in telling of a case history of a soldier suffering from a war neurosis. Some fellow soldiers, as a prank, rolled a bomb without a detonator into his dugout. He could neither retreat from the bomb nor go past it, so he fainted and developed some paralysis. He dreamed frequently of the event until a therapist explained it to him and related it to a dream in which the door of an elevator is blocked by a fierce cat, and "after his re-education in his attitude to cats and bombs is passed fit for general service again" (141–142). Since the man was not permanently cured, Graves posited another solution. The blocking of movement by a threat is clear. Graves extends his inquiry into the life of the man as a boy who had been frightened by a cat, had been to a Puss-N-Boots show, and had worked as an elevator operator. He concluded that bomb and cat "both were a symbol of trench-warfare" and that the paralysis or "shamming dead" was a desperate response to returning to battle (145). Graves's continued discussion of the case study closely relates the cat and the war neurosis to his own life. If the dreamer had been "of German blood on his mother's side so that the fear of being thought a traitor and the regard of his mother's family were continually interacting, then the dreams or the poetry would in the cat-stage be wilder and more incoherent than ever" (146). Having for his middle name Ranke, his mother's maiden name, did cause Graves personal difficulty with his comrades and, as he indicates, severe psychological problems.

Though Graves does not say so, the event with the bomb may well have happened to him. Without doubt, he had the cat dream in his childhood. The nightmares of childhood and warfare joined again in his dreams and in his poem as he indicated in discussing the problem of his German ancestry. To distance himself from the poem and the dreamer, Graves offered five different critical solutions, the last of which is the most relevant to his own poetic:

> But there is a distinction between poetry in which the use of allegory is static, confined to a single consistent theme (as the bomb dream used as an allegory of war and poetry in which a variety of allegories occur) as in the cat dream. (150)

Graves's discussion of poem, dream, and neurosis precisely fits his own imaginative life. Here, again, Professor Scarry's discussion of analogy makes sense. Graves's soldier has retreated to the cosmology of the dream world, this time a child's nightmare. He will extend by analogy experience beyond the momentary and present. And his means in this poem was to look into the personal unconscious. Yet the images of the poem evoke distinctly both childhood and trench warfare. His mention of morphine in "A Child's Nightmare," in other poems, and in Good-Bye To All That indicates how frequently the drug was used. Without doubt, Graves was given morphine when he was wounded. As an officer, he would have carried it with him and, if in need, would not have had to rely on medics. Graves recalled an officer named Hill giving his platoon sergeant five pellets of morphine to deaden the pain of a fatal stomach wound. Always the officers carried morphine for such emergencies (148). Although Graves's poems about his childhood suggest that it was not simple and idyllic, in no other poem does he take us into such violence. The "Cat" is associated with his wounding almost to death and so preserves his use of analogy; but the nightmare figure who stood over him with "straddling legs" and spoke the word "Cat" is certainly human and male, though Graves can only identify him by actions, not by name or features.

As he had associated the telephone with the violence done to him in the war, and the resulting trauma, so did he associate it with the train, which remained in his psyche a symbol of violence. He recalled that violence and his helplessness in "A Child's Nightmare." Though with some catlike features, clearly the creature in his dream is human. Whatever the experience, it was traumatic, and as such was repressed until Graves was once again as helpless as he had been in the nursery. Such a poem does not present childhood as a contrast to war. Instead the poem tells of wounding in the same language, equates the experiences, and moves between the two as if there were no separation. After his marriage, Graves would frequently equate his sexual experience with the traumas of childhood and war. Clearly Graves was "haunted" and would spend years trying to control or ameliorate these hauntings. He would only be partially successful.

Though Graves could not distance the violence and trauma of war in his poems about childhood, in his poems about the regiment and his comrades, past and present, he justified the ways of war to man. Asserting that the war was kept going by politicians and profiteers, Graves separated such actions from those of his comrades and gave to all both benison and praise. When he looked to Roman times, as in "The Legion," he saw men made better by belonging to the Three-and-Twentieth Legion, though "Unsoldierlike, slovenly":

They all try, Strabo; trust their hearts and hands,
The Legion is the Legion while Rome stands,

And these same men before the autumn's fall
Shall bang old Vercingetorix out of Gaul. (36)

In "The Legion," which was published in the English but not the American edition of *Fairies and Fusiliers*, Graves made the past as real and immediate as his present, a talent that would serve him well in such historical novels as *I, Claudius*. And when he re-created Lovelace and the Cavaliers in "To Lucasta on Going to the Wars—for the Fourth Time," Graves admonished the woman to understand that though her man returned to France, he hated war, but laughed and flung an oath not out of courage or fear but simply because "he's a Fusilier, / And his pride sends him there" (17). These two poems, in clear contrast to the poems with childhood and war as subject, glorify the regiment, praise the valor of his comrades, and assert his own willingness to struggle against the foe, restated in the Bunyanesque "The Assault Heroic" where "The dungeon of Despair / Loom over Desolate Sea." The poem ends with a paean to personal bravery in jarring contrast to such a poem as "A Child's Nightmare." Understandably, Graves did not reprint this poem, the flag-waving optimism of which not even Tennyson attempted. Seen as a poem belonging to a collection ostensibly intended by Graves for his comrades and also as an exorcism of ghosts, this poem has value, albeit not poetic value.

In 1917 Graves knew he would be called on to return to France and had to deal with his hauntings. He did so by letting the unconscious empty itself and by putting the best face on battle he could: it would end, and until it did, he would do his duty. Only three poems in the volume offer any escape from thoughts of what he regarded as his inevitable return to battle and from thoughts of his inevitable death. In "Double Red Daisies" and "I'd Love to Be a Fairy's Child," he contrasts childhood with war. In the first, he warns Claire and Ben, brother and sister, not to plant his flowers lest he root them up, not a charitable comment. But in the second, he wrote a simple and idyllic poem about being a fairy's child free of worry and assured of getting "their heart's desire," surely a reference to Yeats's play *The Land of Heart's Desire*. There a priest, Father Hart, and a fairy child vie for the soul of Mary, a young bride. The priest offers the rewards of Heaven for a good life—and mortality. The fairy child offers a land

Where nobody gets old and crafty and wise,
Where nobody gets old and godly and grave,
Where nobody gets old and bitter of tongue,
And where kind tongues bring no captivity; . . . (324)

Graves would have understood the conflict and perhaps desired the young woman's resolution, death in life and life in the never-never land of fairy. He would always feel such a longing for resolution, but would ever write of the only possibility he could accept: mortality that exists in the awareness of the spiritual. On the strength of "I'd Love To Be A Fairy's Child," Graves gave fairies equality with fusiliers in the title to the volume.

Graves, without acknowledgment, expanded his literary influences after the war. He was about to begin his mature writing and would shed, increasingly, the Victorian influence of his father. Steadily, as well, he would withdraw from the Georgians, though he was deeply imprinted by the same view of England and by the same class. Though he had longed to escape jingoism by returning to the trenches, he seems content to have been reassigned to England in February of 1918. At Somerville College, Oxford (then a hospital), he rested from bronchitis and general exhaustion. He would recover from his physical wounds, but he would be informed forever by the accompanying traumas. Badly shell-shocked, he would soon have to negotiate a new world of sex and society and love of a woman, of political entanglements with pacifists and the military. Even with the demons that had streamed out when the door into his unconscious opened, Graves was able, though a young man, to deal persuasively with men of power and significance. If he seemed to stumble with women, that is not so much because of his inexperience as because of his need for a woman to direct his life. He would always be so, and in 1944 would devote himself to the manifestation of that power, a divinity he finally called the White Goddess, the same power he had in 1924 called "the death-white Fay."

Graves looked for patterns within the violence of war and the trauma he experienced. What he found was the developing science of psychoanalysis with its world of the unconscious and its new shamans, such as W. H. R. Rivers. From talks with Rivers, Graves would come to understand the fictive world that was encroaching on the reality that had produced him and then sent him to France. With the analogy, Graves found entree to a world of images and values that existed within his poetry, not in his everyday life. Though the parts of the analogy are drawn from his life, they actually exist together only in his poems. As examples of rhetoric, the poems are simplistic, not even acquiring the distinction of metaphors. The parts remain separate, with their only connection being that the conditions of each respond to the same stimuli: the poet's trauma.

Graves's devotion to the process of psychoanalysis to provide patterns would result in several prose works and many poems. In time, however, he would reject psychoanalysis and the pattern of the analogy to which it led him. He would come to believe that his mind turned to the irrational not because the war had destroyed the credibility of reason, but because the fact of his spiritual life could not be explained by the pattern-seeking of any science. In his war poems, Graves did not find the "one story," but he did become aware of "poetic unreason," a way of being a poet and yet, perhaps, mad at the same time. World War I deprived Graves of his simple faith in the reasoned rhetoric that underlay the Georgians, whom he once regarded as so modern. But Graves would not understand the power of such "unreason" until he experienced the trauma of love.

CHAPTER 3

THE LUNATIC

After the War

Incubus

Asleep, amazed, with lolling head,
Arms in supplication spread,
Body shudders, dumb with fear;
There lifts the Moon, but who am I,
Cloaked in shadow wavering by,
Stooping, muttering at his ear?
Bound in Body, foot and hand,
Bound to lie at my command,
Horror bolted to lie still
While I sap what sense I will.

Through the darkness here come I,
Softly fold about the prey;
Body moaning must obey,
Must not question who or why,
Must accept me, come what may,
Dumbly must obey.

When owls and cocks dispute the dawn,
Through the window I am drawn
Streaming out, a foggy breath.
. . . Body wakens with a sigh
From the spell that was half Death,
Smiles for freedom, blinks an eye
At the sun-commanded sky,
"O morning scent and tree-top song,
Slow-rising smoke and nothing wrong!"

The Pier-Glass

Graves would return to France a last time, posted to the Second Battalion again in January of 1917. As with Siegfried Sassoon, Graves was haunted by the dead and felt guilty for being alive and, since alive, for not being in combat. Clearly unfit for service, he was returned to England after he collapsed: "The major of the R.A.M.C. recognized me and said: 'What on earth are *you* doing out in France, young man! If I find you in my hospital again with those lungs of yours I'll have you court-martialled'" (217).

As was true for Sassoon and many others, Graves was even more wounded emotionally than physically. Ghosts of the dead appeared, and Sassoon wrote of the war intruding even into the peace and quiet of the English countryside in "A Quiet Walk," which he copied into his diary for 1 June 1917. Waking through a Georgian landscape of country lanes, hawthorn hedgerows, blue skies, birds, and breezes, he is shocked out of his musing on the grazing sheep by an "ugly horror":

> A man was humped face downwards in the grass,
> With clutching hands, full-skirted grey-green coat,
> And something stiff and wrong about his legs.
> He gripped his loathing quick . . . some hideous wound . . .
> And then the stench . . . A stubble-bearded tramp. . . . (172–173)

Like the ghosts of dead friends, the tramp brings Sassoon back to the war. Sassoon's diary entry for April 11th records another similar experience: finding in a trench the ten-day-dead body of an English soldier. England would never be the same for Sassoon or for many of the veterans, Graves among them. And even after the Armistice, Graves wrote of seeing the heads of dead comrades on the shoulders of the living. In a poem in the section of *Country Sentiment* (1920) he called "Retrospect," Graves presented his own experience with the ghosts of war and with the guilt that (we can assume) caused him to see them. As with many of his poems about war, he chose not to reprint "Haunted," in which he asked his old friends now dead to leave life to the living, though he knows they will not:

> I met you suddenly down the street,
> Strangers assume your phantom faces,
> You grin at me from daylight places,
> Dead, long dead, I'm ashamed to greet
> Dead men down the morning street. (87)

Graves did not question the authenticity of the ghosts, though at the time he believed the apparitions that appeared in his dreams resulted from his psyche's working out of the problems of battle. Such apparitions as in "Haunted," however, did not come to him in sleep but in waking. Though he would write of his understanding of the apparitions of sleep in *The Meaning of Dreams* (1925), that book would not address ghosts, a constant subject in Graves's poetry for many years.

After he returned from France the last time in 1917, Graves was posted at Somerville College, Oxford. While there he visited Siegfried's friends Lady Ottoline and Phillip Morrell, who lived at Garsington, a manor house near Oxford. The Morrells were pacifists, as were their friends, among whom were Virginia and Leonard Woolf, Robbie Ross, Clive Bell, Aldous Huxley, Lytton Strachey, and Bertrand Russell. Graves observed that "it was here that I first heard that there was another side to the question of war guilt" (307). Also in this company the defining difference between Graves, Sassoon, and the others who fought in France and those who had not was clear. Graves recalled the moral ambiguity, perhaps even amorality, that battle created when Bertrand Russell, probably at Garsington, asked Graves how he would react if he and his men were assigned to break up a strike by munitions workers. If the workers refused to withdraw, would Graves order his men to fire on the workers, and would they obey him? Graves said he and his men disliked the munitions workers and would "be glad to shoot a few," and that they would follow his order to fire even though they and he could agree with Russell that the war was "all wicked nonsense." Russell could not understand Graves's response (220–221).

Graves and Sassoon had enlisted for reasons that later seemed to embarrass them slightly: Graves to put off going up to Oxford, and Sassoon to escape the boredom of his life. Whatever their reasons, the life of the regiment and the experience of war changed them. Graves would always write well of soldiers who did their duty, and he never forgave war profiteers and jingoists. In many respects, Graves remained a patriot throughout his life.

Graves and Sassoon were bound by loyalty to their comrades and to the regiment—and perhaps, as well, by the guilt that they lived while others died. They were not theoretical in their reasons for going to battle. Nor were they theoretical in their objections to the war. With the encouragement of the pacifists gathered around the Morrells (especially Russell), Sassoon decided to publish a letter letting the people in England know the reality of the war, and he did so because he believed the war was being prolonged to increase the profits of industrialists, condemning to death soldiers whose only crime was their sense of duty. His letter changed into a statement in which he refused to support the war effort. As did Graves, Sassoon attributed the continuation of the war as the work of war profiteers. Sassoon spoke for the soldiers whose deaths he saw as unnecessary. His expectation was for a court-martial in which he would reveal the duplicity with which the war was conducted. The charge of treason was a possibility. This letter developed from Sassoon's writing to J. A. Spender, the editor of *The Westminster Review*, a pacifist publication, asking if a statement from a soldier could help bring about peace. With a letter of introduction he visited Bertrand Russell, who in due time helped him with his letter of complaint. That Sassoon was incapable of rational decisions is clear from his vacillation between near suicidal bravery and pacifist outbursts. But he was entranced by the attentions of the elegant intellectuals who gathered at Garsington.

In *The Complete Memoirs of George Sherston* (Sassoon's slightly fictionalized autobiography), he records his pleasure with the attention he received from a philosopher named Tyrrell (Bertrand Russell) and his own respect for the man, a respect not shared by David Cromlech (Robert Graves), who said that the "Pacifists were only meddling with what they didn't understand":

> "At any rate Thornton Tyrrell's a jolly fine man and knows a bloody sight more about everything than you do," I exclaimed. "Tyrrell's only a doctrinaire," replied David, "Though I grant you he's a courageous one."
> (CMOGS 318)

Sassoon sent the letter, which he recorded in his diary on 15 July 1917, to his commanding officer on July 16th. It was read in the House of Commons and published in *The Times*. Copies were sent to several literary and political figures, such as Thomas Hardy, Arnold Bennett, H. G. Wells, Edward Marsh, and Graves himself. Recognizing that his friend was making a decision that would neither serve his own needs nor shorten the war, Graves tried to dissuade Sassoon from making himself liable for court-martial, the intended platform for his statement. Unsuccessful in his argument, Graves, in Sassoon's phrase, did "a bit of wire-pulling." Graves said that Sassoon "should soon find that my Pacifist M.P. wouldn't do me as much good as I expected" (CMOGS 318). Graves arranged for a medical hearing that would find Sassoon's statement the result of emotional and psychological trauma. Sassoon does not even imply that he was ill, but according to Graves,"because he was ill, and knew it, he consented to

Siegfried Sassoon, ca. 1920

appear before the medical board" (GBTAT 233). Graves's discussion of Sassoon's medical board reveals a man already comfortable with the powerful and also reveals his own fragility. Having decided to "rig" the medical board, Graves spoke directly to the captain, a nerve specialist in for the duration, and relied on him to convince the other two doctors, a patriotic colonel and a "reasonable but ignorant" major. When Graves told them of Sassoon's suicidal bravery and of seeing Piccadilly strewn with corpses, he burst into tears three times as he spoke, prompting the captain to observe that Graves should himself be appearing before the board. Graves controlled himself as well as possible in spite of being obviously distraught and nearly overcome with the irony of having to argue "to these mad old men that Siegfried was not sane!" Graves did win the day and was assigned to see Sassoon safely to Craiglockhart Hospital in Scotland, where he would receive treatment from Dr. Rivers. Unfortunately, Graves missed the train, and Sassoon took himself to the hospital (233). Clearly Graves was not well at the time; however, he not only managed to convene the medical board, but to manipulate it and to neutralize a member of Parliament. Nowhere does Graves indicate either how he arranged this feat or how he gained access to the people who had the power to effect it. Graves was barely twenty-one at the time. Though he may well have questioned the continuance of the war, he did not consider adopting a pacifist view, as he explained in a letter of 12 July 1917 to Marsh about his support of Sassoon:

> It would be true friendship for me to heap coals of fire on the head of the dog that bit me by turning pacifist myself but you can be quite assured that I'm a sound militarist in action however much of a pacifist in thought. (BCNYPL)

For Graves to call himself "a pacifist in thought" raises a question about his affiliation with the Morrells and their circle. All were confirmed pacifists: Russell, Strachey, the Woolfs. And Graves was a frequent visitor at Garsington. Later he would publish poetry and fiction at the Woolfs' Hogarth Press. The association with the Morrells was most likely purely social. Introduced by Sassoon into this circle, Graves seems to have been taken with them but never relinquished his own "militarist" views. After his marriage, his visits to Garsington became troublesome since Nancy was not inclined to accept the behavior of Lady Ottoline, a notorious troublemaker for married couples, and would soon refuse to accompany her husband there.

Graves's publications at the Hogarth may well have been simply to get his name before the bright and fashionable in hopes of increasing his readers. Yet he ended his associations with the Garsington circle and the Woolfs by 1927 and does not seem to have renewed them. He would soon after form a relationship with Laura Riding; and they would institute the Seizen Press, which she would have considered equally fashionable as the Hogarth. And Graves was to publish books that made money: *Lawrence and the Arabs* (1927) and *Good-Bye To All That* (1929). Whatever the case, by 1927 Graves clearly did not need or want these fashionable friends.

During his treatment and convalescence at Craiglockhart Hospital, Sassoon came under the care of Dr. W. H. R. Rivers. Rivers would introduce Graves to depth psychology, leading him to see connections between dreaming and writing poetry. This connection was extremely important to Graves, but less so, if at all, for Sassoon. The difference between the two men is readily evident in their poetry. Sassoon writes of the experience in terms that evoke the presence of war, as in "*The Effect*," a poem responding to the comment of a war correspondent that after a bombardment a man told him he had never seen so many dead before. Sassoon rejects the nobility of death as well as its mystery, writing only of the enormity of the violence:

> When Dick was killed last week he looked like that,
> Flapping along the fire-step like a fish,
> After the blazing crump had knocked him flat. . . .(CPSS 87)

Sassoon wrote this poem in the summer of 1917, part of what he called "Hindenburg line material," the area of the war he fought in with the Second Battalion just before he wrote his letter of protest. Sassoon's poems have the bite of fact, as Graves's never do. The war had very different value for Sassoon than for Graves, as Sassoon made clear in *Memoirs of an Infantry Officer* (CMOGS). Sassoon portrayed Graves as David Cromlech, a soldier who "had no use for anti-war idealism and had a strong sense of 'the regimental tradition.'" Yet David had "a first-rate nose for anything nasty." He found the horrible in war, not the heroic as did George Sherston, Sassoon's fictional representation of himself. What Sassoon saw in Graves was a contradiction, not yet a paradox, of emotions, of realities in fact.

Sassoon may well have been right about Graves, for whom war would ever be an unresolved conflict between the bravery of men and the waste of life. But for Graves, the war opened a door into the darkness of the psyche where the daily horrors of war merged with the repressed horrors and ugliness of childhood and, later, of marriage. Graves would be haunted throughout his life by the merged emotions and experiences contained in the images he carried in his psyche. Graves and Sassoon depended on their presence in the war to justify the harm they had done to the enemy and, in their minds, to their own comrades, men they had sent to their deaths. Although Sassoon clung to the hope that the war could in some way justify its destruction through the glorification of bravery, Graves did not hold such views.

But then Graves was not a war poet. Though the war changed his existence, Graves would not spend the majority of his creative life examining it by reliving it, as would Sassoon and, in his own way, Basil Liddell-Hart.

Yet Graves would, by all indications, be a patriot and a dedicated militarist for the rest of his life, and the regiment would never receive censure from him. Though he complained about the war profiteers, he did not record the serious complaints against the government that Sassoon made. Perhaps his friendship with Edward Marsh, a longtime associate of Churchill, made such complaints inappropriate. The war touched Graves through the nastiness of death, not through the glory of dying. And that nastiness was as deeply imbedded in his psyche as in the olfactory memory of Hemingway's Pilar in *A Farewell to Arms,* for whom the awareness of death was of smells: of a ship battened down in a storm, of the mouth of an old woman who goes to the slaughterhouse to drink the blood of the beasts, of a garbage pail with dead flowers, all compounded into the smell of sex and a prostitute left on a gunny sack that had been a bed (254–256). Graves, with few exceptions, wrote not about the nastiness of war, but about his response. So the war became a part of his understanding of himself that he depended on for stability, neurotic though it was, while he was in the army. Immediately after the war, much of his poetry would come from his keeping his neuroses alive and frightening.

As Graves later wrote, many of the soldiers in World War I found that they became poets in the trenches. This was true for Sassoon and even for such a moving poet as Wilfred Owen. Whatever the reason, the war poems of Sassoon and Owen are far more forceful and immediate than any of those by Graves. Oddly, Graves failed to see the real worth of Owen as a poet and wrote to Sassoon on 12 January 1918 that "Owen, I told you, is fearfully uncertain; but he can see & feel, & the rest will be added into him in time." No poem Graves wrote about the war can compare with Owen's "Dulce Et Decorum Est."

> Knock-kneed, coughing like hags, we cursed through sludge,
> Till on the haunting flares we turned our backs
> And towards our distant rest began to trudge.
> Men marched asleep. Many had lost their boots
> But limped on, blood-shod. All went lame; all blind. (1:140)

From the nightmare of the day, Owen and Sassoon escaped to memories of the past or peacetime activities. Even while at Craiglockhart, Sassoon spent time on the golf links, much to Graves's concern, which he voiced in a letter of 13 September 1917: "I want you to tell me honestly are these shell shock fellow patients of yours getting on your nerves? I'd be unhappy if I thought they were: you talk of golf with lunatics, but I hope to

God it's not as bad as that" (BCNYPL). It was as bad as that for Sassoon and had been for some time, not only in his companions, but in his own stability, as Graves asserted in a letter he wrote to Sassoon on 11 January 1917, taking as he frequently did the role of mentor to the older Sassoon. Graves saw Sassoon as so obsessed by "a strong anti-war complex" that he could no longer conceive of a world happier though emptier than the one they fought to preserve. He ended the letter: "Don't send me anymore corpse poems" (BCNYPL). Understandably, the daily horror of the war obsessed Sassoon and filled his writings with its violence and its residue, the corpses. Just as understandably, Graves was unnerved by Sassoon's poems since, clearly, Graves was not well. Graves's turning within of the violence rather than externalizing it indicates the lasting effect the war would have on him. It permanently altered his vision, his understanding, and his reality. Though he might ask to be sent no more "corpse poems," the damage had been done. As Graves continued to assure Sassoon that he wasn't "dotty," he revealed as troubled a mind as Sassoon's in the above letter. Both clung desperately to the hope that when the war ended, the nightmares would end as well. They were wrong, but they did try to regain the order of the past. When Sassoon returned to active service after his brief alliance with the pacifists, he was posted to Ireland. The Irish Rebellion was underway in 1917, yet Sassoon wrote only of hunting with the hounds with a ridiculously conceived stage Irishman named Reilly, who was full of whiskey and begorras.

The war was a violent wrenching of the psyche from which Sassoon may never have recovered. But even in *Sherston's Progress,* which he wrote in 1936, the last volume of his fictionalized memoirs, he remembered in detail the nights and days in Craiglockhart: the night sounds of insomniac officers padding in slippers through the passages which smelled of stale tobacco smoke and of men crying out in their sleep, tormented by dreams of the front line which in the daytime would be discussed with the analyst, only to return with dark when "no doctor could save him," the "lonely victim of his dream disasters and delusions" (70–71). Graves himself must have spent many such nights, especially after the war, for the poetry he wrote after the war is filled with hauntings and sleepless nights, with ghostly visitations and terror. Whether he actually had a "nose for whatever is nasty" or whether his experiences as a child and later as a lover were as traumatic for him as those of war, Graves wrote poetry for ten years after the Armistice that often merged his traumas into single images. In fact, as was also true for the Confessional School of poets, Graves became dependent on his neuroses. He would not be able to control the force of wartime memories and trauma until he was able to fix a being in his experience with the power to traumatize yet not destroy him. This would be the life- and death-giving White Goddess, whose story he would construct from Celtic myth, though driven and directed by his personal needs, desires, and experiences. Such construction, though not the discovery, would come much later, after the breakup of his marriage to Nancy Nicholson, after the departure of Laura Riding, after the arrival of Beryl Pritchard Hodge. It would occur, then, after the healing efforts of three women. And of equal importance, the construction would occur after Graves's real experience of the Goddess, which Catherine Dalton said occurred early in his life.

In *Good-Bye To All That* Graves does not present the young Nancy Nicholson as a likely candidate for goddess, yet she was a good study for one and would be his first muse. Innocent, opinionated, and spoiled, she was a match for Graves, who might be described the same way. Graves was twenty-two and Nancy seventeen when they were married in January 1918 at St. James Church in Piccadilly. She had never before read the marriage service and was horrified by it, though Graves had tempered the misogyny as much as he could. Graves describes the wedding as an overemotional ceremony that may well have been reflected in many other rushed engagements during wartime. Graves was in field boots, spurs, and sword, shouting out responses in a "parade-ground voice," and Nancy was in her silk wedding dress, furious with the ceremony itself and muttering responses (GBTAT 241). Neither Graves nor Nancy had any experience with sex. She was appalled later when she found out how children were conceived and born. Graves recalled: "The embarrassments of our wedding night were somewhat eased by an air-raid; bombs were dropping not far off and the hotel was in an uproar" (241).

The embarrassments may well have occurred. The portrayal of Nancy, though, is off the mark according to Catherine Dalton. Bitter at losing Geoffrey Phibbs to Nancy, Laura Riding used her considerable influence over Graves to have him revise Nancy Nicholson out of *Good-Bye To All That*. In this, Riding was, basically, successful since Graves left a rather predictable portrait of an ex-wife, damning her as a woman who, because of her irrational feminism, could not see the harm done to men in war as incomparable to the harm done women. Catherine Dalton, in her letter of 31 October 1997, rejected the portrayal of her mother as irrational, and also rejected the term "feminist" to describe her. More accurately, said Dalton, she should be called an "equalist," believing everyone should get the same pay regardless of gender, race, class, or age. (At fourteen, Nicholson had received half the normal rate for doing a cover for *Vogue* because she was a minor.) With her talent and refusal to accept conventions blindly, Nancy Nicholson was a beneficial companion for young Graves. But he was always fortunate in his companions and collaborators—whether by choice or chance. Nicholson helped him leave Victorian thought, and Riding helped him leave England. Much of the rest of his life was in the capable care of Beryl Graves.

In *Fairies and Fusiliers* Graves wrote of a need to have a retreat *"From Frise on the Somme in February 1917."* He chose "England in June attire / And life born young again" (38). In *Treasure Box* (1919), his next volume of poetry and his first after being married, he wrote of his need for another escape:

> In my body lives a flame,
>   Flame that burns me all the day,
> When a fierce sun does the same,
>   I am charred away. (65)

Though he longs for caves, brooks, and nooks, anything cool, he knows they cannot diminish an anguish that is spiritual rather than physical, an anguish that comes from within. Love which comes at night destroys him, yet he is renewed by the love of the day. In the morning he is restored, daily, by the morning phoenix that is reborn from the ashes of his "Calcined heart and shriveled skin." Granted, Graves could be describing nothing more extraordinary than post-coital *tristesse*. But as with his memories of childhood and war, sex produced trauma for him. Giving the phoenix a "proud roar" conventionalizes sound, which is but an echo in this poem, probably from battle, but it does not have the power to overwhelm Graves as it did before and would later. His vulnerability appears even in this poem of early marriage and would grow in frequency and force to become a major theme. However, in the early stages of love, his neurosis seems to take a holiday as well. As the sound of battle receded, desire had not the power to burn him or to destroy him, as his friend Robert Frost would observe it could:

> Some say the world will end in fire,
> Some say in ice.
> From what I've tasted of desire
> I hold with those who favor fire. (268)

Yet Graves would soon find the effects of battle and of love to have similar resonances: he is inert, shriveled, and unfeeling, in need of rebirth. Though the war has ended, he is not a whole man as he, perhaps, expected to be. He certainly did not at this time expect marriage to plunge him back into the despair he had experienced in France. His views of love and marriage seem as unrealistic as those of most: passion and spiritual adventure. Fortunately, that is what he got, as so often the wounded have not. Yet always he sensed an inner life more powerful than his ordinary life, and even that ordinary life frequently overwhelmed him.

Graves, as have many, expected marriage and love to aid in his healing. He openly stated the value of his love in the "Author's Note" at the beginning of *Whipperginny* (1923) to explain the focus of *Country Sentiment* (1920) and *The Pier-Glass* (1921):

> *The Pier-Glass,* a volume which followed *Country Sentiment,* similarly contains a few pieces continuing the mood of this year, the desire to escape from a painful war neurosis into an Arcadia of amatory fancy, but the prevailing mood of *The Pier-Glass* is aggressive and disciplinary, under the stress of the same neurosis, rather than escapist. (v)

Graves believed that by 1929, when he published *Good-Bye To All That,* he had escaped from "a painful war neurosis." He never escaped, and in the twenties had no intention of escaping. In *Country Sentiment,* dedicated to Nancy Nicholson, the poems of "amatory fancy" tell of deceit, failure, and haunting. And he is sustained by such "amatory fancy." As he would be later with the White Goddess, so was he in the early days of his marriage with Nancy: dependent on her for direction and health. Yet his love for Nancy does not overcome his war neurosis, nor does Rivers's assurance that he will return to normal when the threat of war is gone. "Retrospect: The Jests of the Clock" expresses the memories that cannot be expunged or repressed:

> When noisome smells of day were sicklied by cold night
> When sentries froze and muttered; when beyond the wire
> Black shadows crawled and tumbled, shaking, tricking the sight,
> When impotent hatred of life stifled desire,
> Then soared the sudden rocket, broke in blanching showers.
> Oh lagging watch! O dawn! O hope-physician hours! (CS 88)

The dreams continue, as does Graves's resolve (and expectation) to return to war, as he says of himself in third person later, in the end of the poem: "Poor fool, knowing too well deep in his heart / That he'll be ready again if urgent orders come" (89). This poem, with its sense of nightmare, evokes the fear and loneliness of war, the continuing trauma, and Graves's unwillingness to exclude war from his experience. Graves was always a patriot, always ready to go again to war. But in the early 1920s, Graves was not ready for the reflective fiction about war of later years, nor was he ready to re-enlist. He was still absorbed (perhaps obsessed) with integrating war into his life. Though he may have hoped to abate the effect of the war trauma, he without doubt understood his growing dependence on his neuroses.

Graves's most effective poetry of trauma, of war, continues to be associative. When he published *The Meaning of Dreams* (1925), he had come to understand why he was drawn to write such poems, as indicated by his discussion of the view of "associative thought" by Freud, Jung, and Rivers. Praising Rivers for his "admirable observations on the mechanism of dreams," Graves was disappointed because the theories of Rivers and others did not consider "not-logical associative thought" to be as "modern and reputable a mode as intellectual thought." Instead they regarded it as a carry-over from primitive thought, "a rather useless survival like the human appendix or the tassel on an umbrella" (56–57). "Associative thought" had allowed Graves entree into his past, perhaps a repressed past, but certainly one that contained violence and disturbance. In the poems in *Country Sentiment,* Graves uses associative thought to understand the disturbances of love, as in "Song: One Hard Look," a poem he reprinted as late as his *Collected Poems* (1975) in a slightly revised form. Graves presents the fragility of his peace of mind and personal security. A smile from his beloved can relieve a "heart that grieves," just as a hard look can shut "the book / That lovers love to see." Though a look seems of small import, Graves makes clear in the poem that life itself is affected by such seemingly small incidents:

> Small gnats that fly
> In hot July
> And lodge in sleeping ears,
> Can rouse therein
> A trumpet's din
> With Day-of-Judgement fears. (25)

The trumpet, of course, recalls the war, which Graves had good reason to believe would end his life. In fact, his life was permanently affected by his "war neurosis," the constant image of which in his poetry was sound. In

"Song: One Hard Look," the buzzing of a gnat that finds its way into a sleeper's ear becomes for Graves the image of the trauma of love. That the maddening sound is inside, rather than outside, his head suggests a physical as well as a psychological problem which most likely resulted from his constant exposure to terrific sounds during battle.

The force of the woman and the resonance of sound in the psyche would remain part of Graves's understanding of life and poetry. But he would not continue after the 1920s with association as a key part of his poetic. Revisions of early poems would make them coherent where earlier association determined form. He would as well reject the associative ties between fear and childhood, suggesting the link to be rhetorical (or psychological) rather than part of his experience. He may well have been right. His early reliance on association was a rhetorical attempt at establishing a basis for art and thought other than the rational. What he wanted was an experience more primitive than reason, and he found it in the merging of the terror of childhood with that of war. Significantly, he removed three lines when he reprinted "Song: One Hard Look" in *Collected Poems* (1975):

> An urchin small
> Torments us all
> Who tread his prickly way. (25)

During the time he wrote *Country Sentiment,* Graves was still concerned with understanding his own childhood through the traumatic resonances it shared with battle. The poems about childhood in *Over the Brazier* and *Fairies and Fusiliers* indicate that he was not motivated to write poems such as "Song: One Hard Look" only because he had daily contact with children since he and Nancy had become parents. The poems written to and about his own children are, generally, free of torment and horror and express the happiness of childhood, which Catherine Dalton mentioned. Graves equates the disturbances of war, love, and childhood with the sound of a gnat in the ear or the scratching of mice at night. Such small sounds clearly upset him. Sound, which figures significantly in Graves's recollection of war, in "One Hard Look" anticipates his later treatment of his neurosis in "The Gnat," and his discussion of the poem in *The Meaning of Dreams.*

Graves published "The Gnat" in his next volume, *The Pier-Glass* (1921). A pastoral which Graves reprinted only twice, the poem tells of the shepherd Watkin, who was driven mad by a gnat that entered his ear and burrowed into his brain. Confused, he thinks his sheepdog Prinny is the cause of his pain and believes he must kill the dog to find release. The insect has "wings of iron mail" and "metal claws." When it leaves him:

> Out flies the new-born creature from his mouth
> And humming fearsomely like a huge engine,
> Rockets about the room, smites the unseen
> Glass of half-open windows, reels, recovers,
> Soars out into the meadows, and is gone. (40–41)

As Graves explains in *The Meaning of Dreams,* the poem was solely inspired by his "war neurosis," a single analogy, not the more complex one in which love figures. Graves, at the time, saw his war neurosis as continuing because of the threat in 1921 of wars in Russia, Ireland, and the Near East. Then believing in Freud and psychoanalysis, he also believed that dream analysis could "cure" him of his "nervous condition." However, set as deeply in his psyche as the gnat in the ear of the shepherd was the belief that curing the neurosis might end his poetic inspiration. To delineate the images as did Graves, "to be rid of the gnat (shell-shock) means killing the sheep dog (poetry) and when the sheep dog is dead the shepherd ceases to be a shepherd and must become a labourer; that is, I would have to give up being a poet and become a schoolmaster or a bank-clerk" (164). Like the shepherd who doesn't go to his minister for advice, Graves never committed himself to therapy. What he did not understand then, and perhaps never, was that his response to shell shock would be permanent. The sound, as Graves wrote, "has many attributes which connect it with a war-neurosis; it holds suggestions of air-raids, of the zero-hour of attack, and of the crazy noise of battle" (164–165). Perhaps the waning of a trauma directly related to the war enabled him to see and discuss it. He did not, however, discuss the waxing trauma of love to which he attributed the symptoms of war: helplessness and vulnerability imaged as distressing and disorienting sound. In discussing the meaning of "The Gnat," Graves wrote of no longer believing in psychoanalysis and the teaching of Freud and Jung, and reflects that thinking dream analysis could cure him had been "silly."

Matters of importance here are, clearly: sound as image recalling a traumatic condition, and Graves's continuing to undergo psychoanalysis after he had ceased to believe in its curative power. The war neurosis would continue for years; and he would associate the trauma of love with sound as well, as in "The Shout." These are concerns of image, theme, and structure in his poetry, ones which would cause his poetry to be incomprehensible to Edward Marsh. Graves, having rejected the rationality of the

Georgians and the fragmentation favored by Eliot and Pound, would create his own audience.

"The Gnat" illustrates his decision. Bucolic in setting and image, yet modern in meaning, it belongs to the interim poetry Graves wrote to free himself of the past before his experience of sexual passion and woman's love carried him to his future. In brief, the narrative of the poem tells of Watkin, who hears a voice that repeats three times: "Creature, be ready!" (38), which he assumes to be a message for him, not for that within his brain:

> A creature like to that avenging fly
> Once crept unseen in at King Herod's ear,
> Tunneling gradually inwards, upwards,
> Heading for flowery pastures of the brain,
> And battened on such grand, presumptuous fare
> As grew him brazen claws and brazen hair
> And wings of iron mail. (38)

In the case of Herod, the "transgression" was that he did not pay sufficient honor to the glory of God. The story is found in Acts 12:21–23:

> 21 And upon a set day, Herod, arrayed in royal apparel, sat upon his throne, and made an oration unto them.
> 22 And the people gave a shout, saying It is the voice of a god, and not of a man.
> 23 And immediately the angel of the Lord smote him, because he gave not God the glory; and he was eaten of worms and gave up the ghost.

Graves was always a careful scholar, though often a willful one, and would not have accidentally mistaken a gnat for a worm in the story of the death of Herod Agrippa I, grandson of Herod the Great. The sound of the gnat was, most likely, in Graves's head, not Herod's. As well, he was always a careful poet and would not use the reference to the death of Herod decoratively. The biblical source indicates not simply Graves's very solid and traditional education but, perhaps more importantly, the course his understanding of himself and his poetry would assume throughout the rest of his life. Graves would look for historical and textual precedents rather than psychological ones. In revising, often rewriting secular and sacred texts, Graves would justify his own poetic commitments.

In "The Gnat," what troubles Graves is not simply his fear of losing his poetic gift, but his presumption that the role of poet must be his primary and central concern. As such, his dedication to poetry becomes his "transgression." Oddly identifying the sheepdog Prinny with poetry, Graves indicates that the shepherd's "transgression" was his devotion to the dog. Later, Graves would say that prose was like a show dog he raised to support his cat, his poetry. Graves's presumption at this time was his insistence on making his living as a poet rather than providing for his family by getting a regular job. He relied a great deal on loans and gifts from family and friends. But the greater presumption was in holding to the neurosis. One can only imagine what life was like for a woman and small children in a cottage with a man who heard voices, saw ghosts, and was terrified by telephones and trains.

Then, too, life was complicated by the visits of military friends, such as Sassoon, and by the addition of T. E. Lawrence in 1920. Although these two friends helped Graves financially, they did not set well with Nancy. She was trying to heal him of his war neurosis, and the visits of his military friends pulled him back to memories of the war. Even before they met, it was clear that Nancy Nicholson and Siegfried Sassoon were unlikely to be friends; but Graves was completely oblivious, as indicated in this undated letter written to Sassoon soon after the wedding:

> Please henceforward regard Nancy as your mother: she'll play the part much better than most & I think, when we settle down, I hope in Chaucer's house at Woodstock where she was born, we will have to make a sort of creche for homeless poets—the Helicon Hotel. (BCNYPL)

Such a view of married life, though understandable, is unlikely actually to exist in everyday life. Perhaps Sassoon would have resented any woman in Graves's life. Though Graves and Sassoon do not seem to have been lovers, Sassoon's homosexuality is clear and was finally evident to Lady Ottoline Morrell. Recognition of his homosexuality ended her ardor but not their friendship. Sassoon's diary entry for Christmas Day 1917 indicates the strength of the friendship between Graves and Sassoon, and makes suspect Graves's motives in marriage to Nancy Nicholson: "Last Friday went to Rhyl to see Robert Graves, and received his apologies for his engagement to Miss Nicholson" (198).

The friendship with Graves underwent many strains, though Nancy (and later Laura Riding) always irritated Sassoon, as seen in this diary entry from 22 April 1925 after he had visited the Graves family, who were staying in London with his sisters "somewhere off St John's Wood Road," a good address then and now. The household bothered Sassoon, filled as it was with pleasant but dull siblings of Robert; with Nancy, whom he found "queer and uncouth," hiding her shyness in "sharp-tongued reserve"; four sleeping children and a collie puppy named Rufty; and Robert complaining of his nerves, though as ever "charming, affectionate and impulsive." The task of making things go during the evening was left, according to Sassoon, to himself, the visitor (234–235). Nancy Nicholson never received better treatment from Sassoon, who saw her as a watchful guard dog to be placated with jam rolls and condescension. But the confusion in a house with a large, young family, pets, and visitors would have been a shock to Graves, who had only known the more limited male-only world. The growing confusion and instability of his marriage would have been so great that no emotions could have been separate and discreet. No wonder his traumas seemed to have multiple sources. In the section he called "Retrospect," at the end of *Country Sentiment*, Graves does escape from the complexity of his life after the war to recall (and to invent) life in the war as simple and clear-cut, a very different retrospective view than he labeled "Nursery Memories" in *Over the Brazier*, those poems equating violence in battle with that of childhood. The poems in "Retrospect," such as "Haunted," indicate the continuing effect of the trauma as well as the care he had to receive from his wife, and indicate as well why a demanding love would be welcome. But more typical of the poems at the end of *Country Sentiment* is "Here They Lie," a short poem praising the war dead in terms that have a patriotic ring quite different from the inward-looking poems. This poem looks at the world outside Graves's own trauma:

> Here they lie who once learned here
>   All that is taught of hurt or fear;
> Dead, but by free will they died;
>   They were true men, they had pride. (91)

Graves had by now learned more of "hurt or fear" than is taught in battle and may well be necessarily nostalgic just to have a fixed, unchanging point. Marriage and fatherhood are changing, living, and in the case of Robert Graves, very upsetting. Both, though, became essential to his healing. And until he admitted the existence of the Goddess, paradox would be an essential element in his writing. Then fear and love would not be contraries, but equal expressions of devotion.

But his war poems had now become quite revisionist. In *Good-Bye To All That* he recalled the actual person he wrote about in "A Rhyme of Friends." She was an old woman named Adelphine who lived close by Noeux-les-mines, a withered and clean old woman who treated him as she would a child (cs 101). As is often true, Graves's view of his poems and the actual statement of the poems are quite different. As poet, he generally inhabited a reality different from his everyday one. His recollection of the poems in "Retrospect" is a significant case. At the time he wrote *Country Sentiment,* he was at Rhyl as an instructor in a cadet battalion, as he recalls in *Good-Bye To All That.* In that recollection of old Adelphine, she is the money-grubbing French woman of the soldier's cliché, not a proxy for motherhood. Though he says he cannot understand why he put in so many lies, he suggests that the search for audience prompted him, which makes little sense since the English would not be receptive to a French woman. He does suggest an answer by analogy. He dedicated the poem to his wife, Nancy Nicholson, and used her rather than children as a way of forgetting the war. As with Nancy, Adelphine was another mother figure, whether she deserved to be one or not (247–248). For Paul Fussell, *Good-Bye To All That* is an exercise in black humor and satire in which Graves catered to an audience he despised to make money (207–208). The retelling of the story of old Adelphine could well be such a case. If so, Graves is fortunate that his readers were not as clever as Fussell, who never exactly says why he likes this book that so offends him.

Graves may well have been responding to the need of a reading public to feel good about the war, echoing their view that England had fought in the right. Or he may have needed the support of a mother figure, calling forth desired traits in her as he would later from other women. Both of his wives would mother him. As he said above, he "used" Nancy to effect his cure. She even had the motherly task of teaching him to wash properly, as he wrote to Sassoon in August of 1918. Once beyond the factual, that *Country Sentiment* was dedicated to Nancy Nicholson, little in Graves's recollection is accurate. Perhaps written for "public delectation," the poems are not "pacifist," as he claimed. Instead, bravery and duty are praised; even the decency of non-combatants is praised, as with Adelphine, who hated the Germans. The "romantic poems and ballads" all tell of the failure and frustration of love. If these are his experiences with Nancy that took his mind off his war neurosis, the marriage must have been intense indeed—intense and traumatic. What seems evident is that Graves could not write poems of simple praise or uncomplicated happiness, themes that would have been expected of a poet writing for "public delectation." Instead, he wrote of hauntings and of violence, public and domestic. Later, probably under the influence of Laura Riding, Graves would denigrate earlier writing by presenting it as contrived, written only for profit and public approval. He did the same with *Good-Bye To All That* and *I, Claudius* when Riding's works failed to match the popularity and success of his, as his brother John implied in his diary. Graves's biography of T. E. Lawrence, *Good-Bye To All That,* and the two Claudius novels provided their income. The Seizen Press provided Riding with a way of publishing her poetry. She accepted Graves's view that she was the superior poet and that his prose books were merely "potboilers" that brought in money (Seymour-Smith 242). Nancy Nicholson's achievements as an artist and her obvious contributions to making Graves a poet never received such notice. She was an illustrator of note, both for her husband and for periodicals such as *The Owl* and *Vogue*. Her daughter, Catherine, remembered her as having a fine critical intelligence that was genuinely important both to Robert Graves and Geoffrey Phibbs.

Marriage and the birth of Jenny in January of 1919 did cause Graves to reorder his priorities somewhat. Graves would always be a devoted father and husband, in his own fashion. However, early in his first marriage, both he and Nancy seemed devoted to each other. In *Good-Bye To All That* Graves explains why he withdrew from possibly dangerous assignments in Ireland. As he sat in his quarters writing a nonsense poem about Babylon and Banbury Cross for Nancy and his daughter Jenny, some companies of the battalion returned as the drums and fifes made the windowpanes rattle with "The British Grenadier." Briefly the war forced itself into his poem but was driven out by the thoughts of wife and daughter: "I had ceased to be a British grenadier" (250). Though Graves decided to resign his commission at once, he could not get rid of his war neurosis as easily as he did his uniform. He would, as well, remain Captain Graves for several years.

His poetry would not change in theme or tone in *The Pier-Glass,* his next volume, which contains both "The Gnat" and "Incubus." However, the volume contains "The Coronation Murder," an attempt at a historical narrative poem that pleased Graves so much he reprinted it often. This poem recalling Victorian England is less representative of the volume than "Return," which tells of Christ's meeting with the scapegoat:

The seven years' curse is ended now
That drove me forth from this kind land,
From mulberry-bough and apple bough

And gummy twigs the west-wind shakes,
To drink the brine from crusted lakes
And grit my teeth on sand. (53)

Though based on the story of Christ's wanderings, the poem recalls as well that seven years had passed since Graves enlisted. This is not a poem simply about Christ, as is evident from the references to English things in the first stanza and continues with "Robin on the tussock sits" and "Cuckoo with his call of hope." The war enters the poem even among the sheep, who keep "[t]roop discipline" (54). Even when on leave in Wales during the war, Graves would look at the countryside with a soldier's eye, considering the placement of troops and lines of attack. Thus, there is no surprise that the quiet and mannerly countryside does not provide the speaker with the peace he needs. Graves, like Christ, cannot use a scapegoat to bear his load. Though he might, in recollection, have thought he used Nancy as such in these poems, he did not—at least not in the manner implied. He did, however, use her in the poems to add dimensions to his neurosis. Love and death are intermingled themes. And he would repeatedly express hope that the emotional violence would end. Yet he does not seem to have been willing to effect such a change, dependent as he was on the neurosis that commanded the sheepdog of his poetry.

Added to the difficulty of this household and the rejection of Nancy by Graves's homosexual friends was the view of Nancy as a feminist in the very male world of postwar Oxford. Graves "was devoted" to Nancy and accepted and respected her views concerning male "stupidity and callousness" even when he himself was the object of her condemnation. Though Nancy's views were strongly feminist for her time, she seems to have been equally concerned with separating Graves from the war. She even forbade newspapers in the house, not only because of mentions of the war but because women were so frequently portrayed in what she considered an abusive way: the need to keep up "the population" or a clergyman's view of women (257–259). When this passage in *Good-Bye To All That* was written, Laura Riding was severely editing Graves's memoir, at least to color his presentation of Nancy Nicholson and, probably, to make his reflections agree with her own views, such as that sex existed only to increase the population, a view voiced by T. S. Eliot as well.

That Graves was influenced by, or at least in accord with, his wife's views on the current and historical mistreatment of women is evident from the course his life and writing would take. Correcting patriarchal misrepresentation of women became a deep commitment for Graves.

Also, though he had two families, sex was never only important for pro-creation. There always remains a trace of the young man who had to gild the lily. Sex was the medium of the Goddess's domination, the poet's enlightenment. And never would Graves be the dominant partner. And in the mid-1940s, Graves would admit his greatest personal discovery, the White Goddess, the being who dominated his view of early society and religion, the goddess who instituted matriarchy on earth. He would devote himself to her cause: the rewriting of literature and culture in terms of goddess worship.

This presence Graves hinted at in 1924, but the metaphor was yet unformed, though he recognized his need, probably urged on by what seems necessary and unrelenting instruction by his wife. The poem "Incubus," which introduces this chapter, brings together the traumas and uncertainties (though no clear distinction between the two exists) of Graves after the Armistice and after marriage. An incubus is a malevolent spirit that visits a woman; but in this case, the incubus visits a man or poet in the persona of a woman.

That the soldier must without questioning "who" or "why" "dumbly" obey recalls Tennyson's "Charge of the Light Brigade," which Graves had every reason to treat with contempt. In fact, most of his poems written during the war present a strong argument against such mindless patriotism, though they accept the sacrifice of lives. Duty in "Incubus" is merged with the demands placed on the Victorian wife, who had no more "judicial" freedom than did the soldier. Though he might have assumed this role in response to Nancy's views, Graves was inclined to accept the domination of a woman even more than of a superior officer. In "Incubus" he places the male in the role customarily reserved for a woman, one in which rape is possible. The poem, though, is from the point of view of the spirit, not the man; for the workings of spirits always drew Graves into an uncanny empathy, as in "The Pier-Glass," in which he assumes the form of a female spirit. In his later years, such interests would bring a great deal of correspondence from people concerned with the occult and witchcraft; Graves was generally not responsive.

Though "Incubus" is clearly an early venture of Graves into the spirit world, more powerful is the terror of the night, so much like the nights at Craiglockhart as described by Sassoon. The incubus who narrates the poem seems sympathetic with the being he torments, yet is compelled to make his visit. The night and its inhabitants in the moonlight haunted Graves until he accepted the possible terror and pleasure. But in this poem, he simply longs for a life "commanded" by light, not by darkness.

The terror of night patrol was still with him, as were the nightmares that came in sleep. Then, too, "woman-love," in Graves's terms, did not bring peace to him; instead, the poems show intensified distress and distrust. As he said above, Nancy distracted him from his war neurosis by substituting the disturbances of love that could overwhelm and probably relieve his distress. Graves in "Incubus" presents the masculine spirit as one which keeps from his poetry that which his pursuit of the feminine enables— even when the feminine was ghostly and frightening as in "The Pier-Glass." In recognizing his poetic gift and inspiration, Graves came to accept his dependence on the feminine, within himself and without, no matter how violent she might be.

The poems in *The Pier-Glass* were a departure from what Graves had just written. He had by then met T. E. Lawrence and visited with him often, sometimes with Nancy for lunch in Lawrence's rooms at All Souls. Mostly they talked about Graves's poetry, especially his new poems, which would appear under the title *The Pier-Glass*. The mood of *Country Sentiment* was breaking down as his "haunted condition" reappeared. He respected Lawrence's suggestions for improving the poems and accepted most of them (GBTAT 269–271).

By 1924, when he published *Whipperginny*, Graves's war neurosis and its hauntings seem to have abated or, perhaps, have been superseded by the demands of being a husband and father. He had gone up to university, St. John's College, Oxford, in 1919, and found himself in the company of men who, like himself, were "old soldiers," veterans of the war in France, who were returning to their old life and dispositions. In an interesting observation Graves revealed why he and his fellow students avoided studying the eighteenth century: it was French, and the soldiers were almost obsessive in their antipathy, swearing they would only go to war again if it were against the French. The German soldier they admired as "the best fighting-man in Europe." Without concern for politics, they believed they had been on the wrong side, allied with their "natural enemies," the French (263). The Armistice not only ended the war but also the feigned agreement with the French. Oxford was populated by its usual eccentrics, such as Gilbert Murray, the classics scholar, who walked up and down the room as he and Graves talked, prompting Graves to ask the source of his obsessive-compulsive behavior, mentioning that he too suffered a like neurosis. Also in Oxford were the veterans, such as Graves, who probably should have been under psychological care. The times had changed quickly, seemingly without reason; at least the old reasons were no longer adequate. And Graves's life had changed quickly as well: children had come in quick succession, and the always fragile marriage began to show the stresses of time and neuroses. Reflecting on the time when their fourth child, Sam, was born in 1924, Graves wrote: "She began to regret our marriage, as I also did. We wanted somehow to be dis-married—not by divorce, which was as bad as marriage—and able to live together without any legal or religious obligation to live together" (268). They regretted having conformed to a social imperative they did not ac-cept. Theirs was a bohemian life in many respects, politically and socially. But the strength of Nancy's objection is evidenced by her reluctance to be a party to a divorce because she would not accept the name Graves, as was required under British law (Seymour-Smith 361–362).

Predictably, the war continued to be part of their lives, try as they did to avoid it. At Nancy's entreaty, Graves refrained from mentioning the war if at all possible, surely difficult for a man obsessed with it. And they lived in Islip, where the villagers called him "Captain." Then, too, destitute ex-solders came by often to sell odds and ends. They always got a cup of tea and some money. And Graves made yearly train trips (calling forth again the horror of his wounding) to the medical board to verify his disability, neurasthenia. These trips recalled the trip to Rouen and brought back the nightmare (GBTAT 285). This was 1921, and they had moved to World's End Cottage at Islip. They seemed happier away from Boar's Hill, known around Oxford as Parnassus because of the number of poets who lived there. Robert and Nancy had lived in a house they rented from John Masefield and his wife, and Robert sat in the council and played on the village football team (earning a bad reputation for rough play). Ostensibly, all was healthy—except the terms of the marriage and Robert's health.

The poems in *Whipperginny* were written during this time and show Graves more in control of himself than he had been. The dreamlike poems are not nightmarish, nor are the remembrances of war. What he wrote about men and women is either cynical, as in "Richard Roe and John Doe," the story of a cuckold, or, as with "Unicorn and the White Doe," cast in such mythological terms as to be untroubled by mere mortal dalli-ances and failures. Graves was more detached, especially in the last half of *Whipperginny,* and he reflected in the "Author's Note" to the volume that "the appearance of a new series of problems in religion, psychology, and philosophy" did not carry with them the "emotional intensity" of poems essentially concerned with the traumas of love and war (v). These interests in "religion, psychology, and philosophy" proceeded from a more reflec-tive than emotional inquiry into such traumas. Steadily, Graves began to substitute detached reflection for the "emotional thinking" that had grown from his method of analogy. He would soon, though, eliminate "psychology" from his triumvirate and elevate history as he began his life-long inquiry into matriarchy and the authority of woman.

Graves had by this time also become more reflective and less emotional about war. His memories had diminished, at least in the poems, to asides, as in "The Sewing Basket," a poem he wrote to accompany a wedding present from his daughter Jenny Nicholson (the daughters had Nancy's last name, the boys had his) to Winifred Roberts. In the button box were a variety of buttons and "the badges of a Fireman and a Fusilier" (49). Graves had settled into peace, troubled though it was on the personal level, as he shows in "A History of Peace," which reflects on the life of Henry Reece, a champion of peace:

> Henry was only son of Thomas Reece,
> Banker and sometime Justice of the Peace,
> And of Jane Reece who Thomas kept in dread
> By *Pax Romana* of his board and bed. (39)

With such a character as Thomas Reece, Graves reveals his own wife-induced concern with the treatment of married women in the postwar as well as the Victorian times, and indicates his growing distrust of the patriarchy. This distrust may well have been the reason Graves ignored his father's concern with his son's career and his own slighting of his grandfather in *Good-Bye To All That*. So angered was Graves's father that he wrote his own autobiographical response to his son's book and called it *To Return To All That*. Adding intensity to Graves's dislike of the traditional role of men was his view that the war was caused and continued by men such as Reece for their own personal profit. Though he would soon take a pacifist stance, Graves would never abandon his loyalty to the regiment and his respect for his comrades, dead and alive.

Other poems in *Whipperginny* tell of war and the role of old men and religion, such as "A Crusader" and "Reversal," but they add little to understanding Graves's new, more settled appraisal of war. "The Lord Chamberlain Tells of a Famous Meeting," however, considers the role of politicians without Graves's usual rancor. The Kings of East and West meet, much as would spies, which in fact they were. Disguised from all but themselves and the Chamberlain (East's man), they played at cards in a low tavern and discussed the fate of the world (44). The Lord Chamberlain cautions his listeners not to believe what is conveyed to them by "credulous annalists," "approved biographers," "elegant essayists," "vagabond dramatists," or "allegorical / Painters"; instead, they should believe only one who was there. This tale resembles by anticipation T. E. Lawrence's own disguise when he enlisted in the British Tank Corps in 1926 under the assumed name of T. E. Shaw, which is not to indicate that Graves was prescient. T. E. Lawrence certainly assumed disguises and dealt with figures of great personal and political power. He would have told Graves of these, being the man he was, and he was probably even in the early twenties thinking of his own biography. In 1927, Graves would write one of the early biographies. Then Graves, also, knew John Buchan and his writings about spies and world politics. Buchan's novels about the character Richard Hannay were based not only on his friendship with spies but also on his own experience. In 1916 he was a major in the Intelligence Corps and in 1918 was appointed Director of Intelligence. He was a member of Parliament for the Scottish Universities and was Governor-General of Canada when he died in 1940 (Buchan xvii). These two men were close enough to Graves to be among those who recommended him for the professorship at the new Royal University in Cairo, which Graves held for less than one year. Graves moved in heady circles for a young, impoverished poet. He would have known well what one felt like in the presence of greatness, probably very much as did the Lord Chamberlain at the end of the poem. The Chamberlain, who narrates the poem, recalls this meeting between East and West as "the noblest" he had ever seen. The power of the two men was understated by disguise and by their subdued, indeed inconspicuous, parting from each other. Nevertheless, the Chamberlain "trembled," knowing that he had witnessed a "turning moment in world history, and trembled knowing that 'these things must be.' " The rancor with which Graves earlier dealt with politicians and figures of state is absent here, replaced by fear and awe with no hint of irony. By the time this poem was written, probably in 1923, Graves's presentation of his political views had changed dramatically, though not with any constancy. His and Nancy's affiliation with socialism, and communism, can be explained by admitting their rebellion from the conservatism of their parents; Graves's acceptance of Labour was simply because as a member of the county council at Islip, he had offered World's End as a meeting place to Labour members of the council.

Other changes as striking, though briefly held, would appear when Graves became conversant with Basanta Mallik, a Hindu lawyer who had assisted in the formation of a treaty that led to Nepal's independence from Britain. He was sent by the Maharaja to England to study "British political psychology" to help in dealing with future difficulties between Nepal and India. After eleven years in Oxford, Mallik had become a philosopher, and so fond of the British that he had no desire to leave (Seymour-Smith 403). In response to discussions about philosophy and ethics, Graves used notes from Mallik to compose *Interchange of Selves,* which he published as part of *Mock Beggar Hall* with Leonard and Virginia Woolf at the Hogarth Press. They certainly would have approved of the ethical pacifism.

Graves's headnote to *Interchange of Selves* describes the play as *(An Actionless Drama for Three Actors and a Moving Background. Dedicated by the author, Basanta Mallik, to the Lady Cecilia Roberts. In part re-Englished by Robert Graves).* As Martin Seymour-Smith observed: "Actually Graves, in his temporary enthusiasm for Mallik, got him to write a play on lines he suggested, and then completely rewrote it. Its message is that all conflict is evil, that stoical endurance is the only solution" (115). The prologue is a discussion between "The Philosopher and The Poet" after which there are three scenes involving three characters: Mysticus, Liberalis, and Practicus. Although the "three men change character like chameleons, let the historic continuity of each individual be apparent throughout" is the aim of The Poet. Similarities exist between *Interchange of Selves* and such Symbolist plays as *Axel* by Count de Villiers de l'isle Adam: the lack of action, the abstraction of character, and the intent to discuss philosophic propositions. Graves was not successful in following either the Symbolist models or maintaining the "historic continuity of each individual," if he actually intended to do either. Characters do not have identifiable differences, except for broad differences in ideas.

For instance, Liberalis and Practicus disagree about the importance of common sense with reference to the war. Liberalis distrusts common sense, believing it to be only a tool of "the old villains," who left unrealized the goals of the young (44). Practicus, on the other hand, sees common sense as the only way to arrive at a practical solution to the problems raised by the war. Barbarism and civilization, good and evil, the rhetoric of war, are for Practicus, as for Graves in *Good-Bye To All That,* smoke obliterating the real issue: economics and a clash of interests. Graves condemns Liberalis in his own speeches, which approve purging the community of troublesome members. But to Practicus is given the last speech, a reversal of his earlier praise of common sense:

> I never dared to plunge into the mysteries of life before. I suspected
> witchcraft there; all the world outside the span of sense was ghostly,

uncanny to me, and if anybody tells me that my semi-prophetic speech only makes the evil confirmed, rooted in its place, I may not know what to say to meet the charge. (56)

Graves's condemnation of the unexamined following of common sense in the speeches of Liberalis matches his own distrust of what the people at home had set for the young of his generation. Far more than offering a critique of common sense, Practicus relocates truth, as Graves had done, in the spiritual, witchcraft or no. Graves would not abandon common sense entirely, but would render unto the bank what was Caesar's and unto the Goddess his poems.

In this play, Graves covers the spectrum in assessing the causes of the war: from economics to the inherent violence in the species to the involvement of evil witches. None of these seems a particularly likely conclusion for a Hindu lawyer, but they would have appealed to a wide range of pacifists in England at the time. For whatever his reasons, Graves was assuming a role that would have currency within the pacifist community and chose for publisher the Woolfs, who were committed to the pacifist cause. The pacifist stance and the characters and themes of the poems would not continue, and Graves would not find reason to reprint the poems—inhabitants of a fictive world he visited only briefly. He readily took up residence in fictive worlds, as he did in the futurist novel *Seven Days in New Crete* (1949), published in the United States under the title *Watch the North Wind Rise*. Graves wrote this story of a poet taken to the future with a witch riding on his hair in 1947 in a Barcelona hospital where his son, William, was being treated (Seymour-Smith 421–423). In his historical fiction, Graves seems as well to be an inhabitant who remembered stories, not an author who invented them. Graves had the capacity to exist persuasively for his readers (and for himself) in times other than his own present.

After the war, Graves and his family lived a happy, though penurious, life. The war was steadily reduced to traces in the poetry, but the neuroses it caused remained to inform Graves's "mind-life." More than imagination, more than creative insight, this life brought Graves in touch with a spiritual world complete with hauntings and spirits capable of causing death or giving life. The poems present them as part of his reality. Significant and necessary, they may be extrapolations from his life and marriage, the perceptions of a troubled mind, or a reality—the last a possibility Graves himself would only fearfully suggest.

Graves played a variety of roles in these poems: submissive lover, observer of the passing political scene, and old soldier. There is no jelling of all into one, suggesting contrary demands on him: to please public, sponsors, and wife. What is clear is that the poems suggest a creative mind more complex than his biography indicates. And all may well come from his understanding of the necessity for power within both personal and public life. His personal life provided his primary understanding of the awe and fascination that would become the one story of his poetry and the impetus for his research and inquiry into myth.

CHAPTER 4

THE LOVER IN THE NURSERY

Children of Darkness

We spurred our parents to the kiss
Though doubtfully they shrank from this—
Day had no courage to review
What lusty dark alone might do—
Then were we joined from their caress
In heat of midnight, one from two.

This night-seed knew no discontent,
In certitude his changings went;
Though there were veils about his face,
With forethought, even to that pent place,
Down towards the light his way he bent
To kingdoms of more ample space.

Was Day prime error, that regret
For darkness roars unstifled yet?
That in this freedom, by faith won,
Only acts of doubt are done?
That unveiled eyes with tears are wet
They loathe to gaze upon the sun? (14)

In *Whipperginny,* Graves observed that "much trench poetry" was written by men not "poetically inclined," often by officers to address the conflict between their unexpressed love for the men they commanded and the also repressed fear of "the horrible death that threatened them all" (37–38). For Graves, such conflict and suppression was the same as that of boys who suddenly become aware of sex yet have scant opportunity to experience it and limited ability to express its power. Here, Graves strongly expressed the ties between the trauma of battle and of sex.

Although World War I did not serve to make Graves "poetically inclined" and was not his muse, his observation does succinctly categorize the poetry he published in *Over the Brazier*. It also indicates why Graves's war poetry lacks the immediacy and power of his later poetry and why the poems Graves wrote during the war express neither the horror nor the outrage that characterize the poetry of Wilfred Owen and Siegfried Sassoon. He accepted the Victorian world of his parents so well imagined by Stevenson in Dr. Jekyll, the scientist who respected the proprieties of his society yet turned into what he denied himself to consider. Robert Graves worked for his prizes, accepted the course he would follow from public school to university, accepted the public schoolboy's love for another boy, accepted the bullying and discrimination so much a part of the public school. In brief, he accommodated himself to the world in which he lived, a world of unquestioned cause and effect. If the great Queen ruled the Empire, Aristotle ruled the minds of her subjects: reason and predictability were the essence of reality. And the task of the poet was to sing, without irony, of a world in which all is right, in which the past succumbs reasonably to the future, "lest one good order spoil the world," to quote from the dying words of Tennyson's Arthur.

For the Victorian poets who had tamed the Romantics' awe, Nature was predictably tame as an English garden filled with Georgian poets, scones, and tea. The woods were green, the air was sweet, the sounds were gentle and melodious. At night arose "The Jolly Yellow Moon" as light faded in the west before a "sunset red as wine" (OB 10). Here, Graves's diction is the watered-down Romanticism a schoolboy would have inherited from the Victorians. The reason Edward Marsh and the Georgians came to exist is clear in these schoolboy verses. English poetry was bankrupt. Yet never would Graves, or the Georgians, completely abandon the circumscribed reality of the privileged classes: the public school and the university commons under an English sky, and often the regimental mess. In *A Survey of Modernist Poetry* (1928), Graves did not address such concerns, probably because they are indelible parts of his poetic. Instead, he characterized Georgianism by traits, most of which were clearly evident in his own poetry written during the war: "Nature and love and leisure and old age and childhood and animals and sleep and other uncontroversial subjects" (119). Take away the hauntings and the war, and much of Graves's poetry of the twenties fits this paradigm.

In retrospect, the Georgian world is for us as Graves saw it: a retreat from the mechanized hell of World War I and its progeny, the inhumanity of a mass-produced culture:

War-poetry was Georgianism's second-wind, for the contrast between the grinding hardships of trench-service—which as a matter of fact none of the early Georgians experienced—and the Georgian stock-subjects enumerated above was a ready poetic theme. (120)

However unconsciously, Graves's psyche and poetic during the war and the twenties articulated a conflict that rejected the answers of the Georgians just as much as the answers of his father. Though during the war he was still a schoolboy with an "unerotic" crush on a younger boy, Graves was a soldier in a war no one could describe. Though he adhered to the modulated changes of the Georgians, Graves was becoming a different poet from his idol, Brooke. And he would steadily move away from the poems with reasonable narratives so much admired by Marsh. The war was shaking all but his dreams; and in time, they too would change. The reality of the nastiness of the war would be in conflict with the remnants of peace.

"1915" is resonant of Keats's "To Autumn," so evocative of the Englishness of the season:

And full-grown lambs loud bleat from hilly bourn;
Hedge-crickets sing; and now with treble soft
The red-breast whistles from a garden-croft; And gathering
    swallows twitter in the skies.

The traces of Keats would come naturally from Graves's education, and he carried with him at this time a copy of the Everyman edition of *The Poems of John Keats,* inscribed by his father "To Robbie R. Graves" and given to his son in 1915. The gift is a predictable one since young Graves's poetry showed such influence from Keats and since Keats so represents a poetic (though one tamed by the Victorians) that his father would have admired. Yet the poems Graves wrote in this copy of Keats's poems, as well as most of the other poems in *Over the Brazier,* depart from anything his father, Marsh, or probably even Keats could understand: life and death deprived of wonder, beauty, or mystery. Yet Graves, when he first found himself to be a soldier, could not let go of the familiar past. "1915" piti-ably clings to the idea that he and the boy he referred to as "Dick" had a pure and courtly love. I think that Graves was as innocent and deluded as he described himself in *Good-Bye To All That.* Heterosexual, he lived only in a single-sex society until he married Nancy Nicholson. Public schools and then the army provided opportunity for any form of sexual experi-ence, yet he was a virgin until he married. The persona of "1915" appears again in "Familiar Letter to Siegfried Sassoon" (1916). He anticipates the idealized life he and Sassoon will share after the war, a life of poetry writing and childish travel:

> Hobnobbing with the Changs and Mings,
> And doing wild, tremendous things
> In free adventure, quest and fight,
> And God! what poetry we'll write! (*Poems [1914–1926]* 56)

Graves first published this poem in *Poems (1914–1926)*, but as his headnote to the poem indicates, it had been written much earlier: "*From Bivouacs at Mametz Wood, July 13th 1916.*" The persona of this poem

Edward Marsh (1915)

could be described as naïve or innocent, not dissolute or erotic as one might expect from a soldier or someone shaped by the English public school.

Graves seems to have been as unaware of or unconcerned with Sassoon's sexuality as he was of the possibility of his own sexuality. Even his marriage with Nancy Nicholson distanced reality, both sexual and social, since he fully expected her to be "mother" not only to him but to his friends as well—whether or not they wanted mothering or Nancy wished to mother them. As with the poem to Dick, "Familiar Letter to Siegfried Sassoon" is quite childish, not even adolescent, in creating and clinging to stories an adolescent with any experience of the world would be too self-conscious to write. The naiveté reflects both Graves's youth and inexperience, a cruel reminder of how young were many of those who fought in France. Graves held to these childish fantasies to protect himself from the grisly reality of the war. But in "1915" being "knee-deep in snow and mud" (OB 30) interrupted his imaginary world. As much as anyone's, Graves's childhood and youth were the stuff of *A Child's Garden of Verses,* and such horrors were not found under a child's bed, in the corners of the nursery, or on the playing fields of Charterhouse.

Yet in that volume of Keats's poetry Graves carried with him to France, he wrote early drafts of poems. Three of them he published together in *Over the Brazier* with the title "(Nursery Memories)": "I.—The First Funeral," "II.—The Adventure," and "III.—I Hate The Moon." Each has an italicized subtitle providing an analogical reference to the war. The first poem recalls when he and his sisters found a dead dog with a swollen belly like that of the Boche in the fragment attached to his letter to Sassoon. But the end of the dog is very different from that of the Boche and the dead man on the German barbed-wire barricades. No one buried the dead man, but Robert and his sisters were concerned with burying the dog because in their experience the dead were buried (24). After the burial, they prayed for the dead dog, a great deal more than the short shrift given the dead in battle. The second poem tells of a boy who kills a tiger outside his shack, though the body disappears, presumed to have been dragged home by its mate. The note to this poem gives its source: *"(Suggested by the claim of a machine-gun team to have annihilated an enemy wire party: no bodies were ever found however)."* Graves's retreat into a nursery tale, though, is incomplete:

> But, anyhow, I killed him by the shack.
> 'Cause—listen!—when we hunted in the wood

> My brother found my pointed stone all black
> With the clotted blood. (25)

The detail of the "clotted blood" would come from battle, not from the nursery. In the third of the nursery memories, Graves is unable to escape from his present to the partial security of the nursery. He explains in his note that "III.—I Hate The Moon" was written *(After a moonlight patrol near the Brickstacks)*. No nursery memory or tale draws him away from the terror he felt under the glare of the moon while crossing no-man's-land. This conflicted view of the heavens, finding dread in beauty, resembles much that will characterize the images of Modernism, such as Eliot's paradoxical opening of "The Love Song of J. Alfred Prufrock":

> Let us go then, you and I,
> When the evening is spread out against the sky
> Like a patient etherized upon a table. (3)

Though Graves was not made a poet by the war, an argument (such as this one) can be made that the war made him an English Modernist. Graves shared the views of Modernists such as Joyce and Eliot (perhaps even Pound, though I would not say so if Graves were alive), though much of his sense of identity came from English sources, not Continental ones. As was true for the Georgians and the Imagists, Graves believed the language of poetry he inherited was dead, lost in a past that did not understand the age midwifed by Freud and orphaned by World War I. Sweet reason had lost both appeal and value in a reality explained by association. Marsh may have felt Graves abandoned all sensible poetics with *The Feather Bed* in responding to the irrationality of postwar life; instead Graves was simply reacting to what other writers, such as Joyce, had seen more than ten years before: a reality of moral and psychological instability, and a literature dependent on stability.

Graves, however, did not abandon all he knew. In fact, he gave up very little—in spite of his celebrated *non serviam, Good-Bye To All That.* He formed his poetic from the English tradition, starting with John Skelton and continuing through to Hardy, though he rejected the Victorians and the Augustans. He maintained English verse forms, even insisting on capitalizing the first letter of each line. His poetry never left the English countryside. And he never denied that the role of poet was unimportant, as did Pound and Eliot when they said only the poem was important. Graves was not part of the new professional intelligentsia, though he knew them all. He never wanted to make money as a poet and never wanted to be in

anyone's employ: a difficult role. Although his life was every bit as bohemian as Ezra Pound's, Graves was an English eccentric, and not an international one because his exile never really rang true. He was happy to read
a poem, along with other poets, at Southwark Cathedral in 1972 to raise
money for a Shakespeare Birthday fund and in the course of the event to
instruct Dannie Abse on music, art, and Southwark Cathedral:

> Eventually it was my turn to walk the twenty-two yards to the scaffold
> and face all those seated figures in the soaring, elongated nave (rebuilt,
> I think Robert Graves said, in 1897 to replace the, er, 13th-century
> nave destroyed, er, in 1838.) (*Conversations* 172)

Graves would maintain his friendships with Marsh and Sassoon, after predictable disjunctions, and would continue to be familiar with the important political figures of his day, such as Churchill. But as writer, he was
more of his own age than theirs.

Graves saw in war what Eliot saw in peace: trauma opening the door
to a spiritual reality of paradox and despair. As in Eliot's poem, so in
Graves's. The moon (or the evening) is an emblem, or icon, in which despair has replaced the earlier "jolly" cast. Later, the Moon Goddess would
inspire in Graves the same sense of threat, and he may well recall in her
face the moon over France. In "I Hate The Moon," he executes a personal
and simplistic restoration of meaning to an icon he had come to believe
had been misinterpreted. Throughout his writing, Graves would correct
the misinterpretation he came to call "iconotropy," the intentional misin-
terpreting of an icon's real (i.e., traditional or original) values. Graves's
propensity to look beyond his immediate reality may be significant here.
But the reality of the war and his own childhood memories are para-
mount, as he indicated in a prose piece called "The Dead Dog," which he
sent to Edward Marsh on 10 June 1915. Behind the front lines of battle
and feeling safe, he looked through a window at familiar stars. Drifting
back to childhood, he recalled when he and his siblings found the dead
dog of his poem:

> That had been the first time he'd known what "dead" meant, but at
> the end of the same summer a little boy in a red jersey called Douglas
> had told them that he had just come up from the shore & the fisher-
> men were bringing in a dead man from the waves: he was all swelled
> up too like the poor dog & his face was quite ate up by shrimps. . . .
> All that was ages & ages ago in the days when Heaven was paved with
> Acid-drops & a penny was incalculable wealth & dream & life were

inextricably muddled & the Red balloon dream used to come every night for a week & the Giant Oak used to scream softly on two notes in a dull flat voice for years & years till he nearly went mad—in the days before he had any little brothers. The cold chill of death had blown into this courtyard too, colder & colder till he shivered & ran through the archway & fell flat on his face in the road gasping with horror: & none too soon, for with a great roar the shell struck & burst on the very spot where he had been dreaming. (BCNYPL)

In this prose piece, as in "I Hate The Moon," he lets the stars remain benign, needing some touchstone, some memory to keep the sound and feel of war from becoming his only reality. Understandably, he would send this piece recalling the England of his childhood to Marsh. Even at this time, however, his thought was moving in ways that would later irritate Marsh. The reasonable narrative is losing to one of accident, coincidence, and irrationality. Although no one then understood the effects of long periods of unrelieved battle, the necessity for peace and quiet after battle is clear in Graves's poems, as in "Limbo." The revised version of this poem, published in the 1920 edition of *Over the Brazier,* retains the "cornland," the "horses," and the "babies" but becomes far nastier as Graves prefaces the return to peace with these images from the trenches:

When rats run, big as kittens: to and fro
　They dart, and scuffle with their horrid fare,
And then one night relief comes.

What is important about this revision, though, is Graves's continued reflection on the disgusting and horrifying aspects of the war after the Armistice. Whether Graves revised the poem for the sake of a wider audience or to accommodate his own dreams is moot. The experience remains.

Because of its linear narrative and attention to detail, this poem seems more a record of Graves's experiences than the nursery recollections, those bruises of battles. But the title of this poem suggests that he does not believe he can ever live as he had before: caught between Heaven and Hell with no hope for redemption. His Hell is battle, and the only Heaven he knows is a past to which he cannot return, which may never have existed. The images of the last three lines are like memories of illustrations in a book read in the nursery, distant and idealized. The book he actually recalls, however, did not provide him with idealized and happy memories, instead a deep bruise. In 1918, Graves published in *The New Statesman* a poem called "The Picture Book" in which he recalled a nursery maid from a family vacation in Germany, a Fraulein Spitzenburger, who terrified him with stories from "a German book." The nurse read stories that began innocently enough, then turned violent with the killing of animals and children, the murder of wives by husbands, the burnings of towns. And when young Robert cried, she laughed and picked her teeth. Intimidated and crying, he went to bed:

> And lying in my bed that night
>   Hungry, tired out with sobs, I found
> A stretch of barren years in sight,
> Where right is wrong but strength is right,
>   Where weak things must creep underground,
>   And I could not sleep sound. (81–82)

The poem proceeds from the same analogous thinking as did the earlier "Nursery Memories" to express the damage and horror of the war through the terror of childhood memories. But in "The Picture Book," Graves draws war and peace close, for the image of the child unable to sleep frighteningly conjures up his experience in battle. Often officers drank whiskey when they had to go without sleep, most likely to nightmarish results. Graves only reprinted this poem in *Country Sentiment*. When assembling poems for *Poems (1914–1926)*, he explained to Sassoon in a letter of 26 September 1926 why he chose not to reprint "The Picture Book": "I don't like it at all: partly because of its anti-German sentiment, partly because it's not very strong in the first three verses." In the first three verses, Graves made clear the maid was German; the other verses deal only with his fear, a deeply imprinted one. Probably, he did not need to revise this poem because he had other nursery tales as strong, ones intentionally structured by analogy. He had no headnote telling of war for "The Picture Book," and in this poem he moved into fear deprived of rhetorical tampering.

The three poems gathered together as "Nursery Memories" do not separate the images of peace and war as do "1915" and "Limbo" or even "The Picture Book"; they do not offer an idealized world as a resting place for the bruised psyche. After talks with Rivers, Graves discussed poetry and dream as having manifest and hidden meanings. In these three poems, the hidden meaning is that childhood held horrors, real or imagined, that battle and shell shock forced him to recall. The nightmare of the day finds familiar fears in the hidden memories, which ease the war-troubled poet. Childhood has been lived through; perhaps war would be lived through as well.

Two years after the Armistice, in *Country Sentiment*, Graves's anxiety and trauma had not lessened, though Rivers had predicted they would when the threat of war had ended. The reasons the terror remained are tangled, as "A First Review," the last poem in *Country Sentiment*, notes but does not explain:

> *Love, Fear and Hate and Childish Toys*
> *Are here discreetly blent;*
> *Admire you ladies, read you boys,*
> *My Country Sentiment.* (104)

Here Graves clearly equates the traumas of childhood, war, and love. Most troubling is to look for the common denominators: helplessness and violence. Both color much of his writing, and he works to accommodate their presence. With the memory of the war a constant because of visits from his friends, Graves's war neurosis would continue long after his anticipated recovery. And, of course, neither Rivers nor anyone else had enough experience with such neurosis to understand how it could linger and reoccur, the now well-established flashback of post-traumatic stress disorder.

In war, Graves discovered not only comradeship and his natural ability for strategy but a doorway into the unknown, into a reality not ordered by reason and predictability. Such understanding did not come during battle, though, but was "recollected in tranquility," in the English countryside during a time of peace. Though no Wordsworth, Graves knew of powerful emotions recollected in a peaceful countryside, as when:

> Four collier lads from Ebbw Vale
> Took shelter from a shower of hail,
> And there beneath a spreading tree
> Attuned their mouths to harmony.
> (CS 96)

They sang the Welsh song "Sospan Fach (The Little Saucepan)" in Mametz Wood, creating for themselves and Graves a land without metal hail and thunder from guns. The conflict in the scene creates a disturbing poem and recalls a memory that removes tranquility. Graves's memory of war in *Country Sentiment* brings a terror only suggested by the poems he wrote during battle. So stunned by the experience, he had clung to reason lest he lose it, had clung to the past lest the present become all, had clung to dreams when reality was nightmarish. And when the dreams of peacetime were replaced by the nightmares of wartime, Graves sought comfort and ease in his life as husband and father, but without success.

Because the dreams and memories of war would not leave him, Graves followed them and found other dragons he probably thought were long since abandoned with the toys of the nursery and the demons who lived under the bed and in the closets. With Dr. Rivers as his Virgil, Graves went into the hidden world of the unconscious. The images of war mingled with those of childhood and with those of love and sex, which a Freudian such as Rivers would have seen as inevitable. Again, on the level of manifest meaning, Graves saw in the war the abuse of both children and women, and brought them literally into poems, as in "Give Us Rain":

> But the Flags fly and the Drums beat, denying rest,
> And the children starve, they shiver in rags.
> (CS 39)

Such a poem W. H. Auden (who so admired Graves) may have read and remembered when he wrote in "Epitaph on a Tyrant" (80): "When he scowled the little children died in the streets." The stories and poems of past wars have a grim similarity of flags and armies and of the dispossessed. In the above lines from "Give Us Rain," Graves describes a war that could have been fought in Homer's Troy or the United Nations' Bosnia. In all, mothers have cautioned their daughters to avoid soldiers, and fathers have slapped their sons on the back. And those sons have accepted and celebrated a reality such as the offensive of the Somme, where Graves was left for dead.

The connections Graves made between the battlefield and the nursery are, clearly, of two kinds: observations of the effect of war on children and associations between the terror he felt in the nursery and on the battlefield. In the first, he recalls scenes in which children and women are injured, as in "Give Us Rain." As Graves undoubtedly did, we must feel pity for those children; and we must, as well, recognize that such abuses will continue as long as there are wars, as long as children are helpless. But our response is aroused not by the poem, but by images apart from the poem of children starving, victims of war and neglect. The poem itself does not arouse such feelings; the images are simply codes for an experience other than what the poem offers. The reader is expected to provide details for the abstractions of flag, peace, and rags. Graves exercised, once again, good sense and taste in not reprinting it.

Even in *Country Sentiment*, Graves advises his readers to look for the less obvious meanings of seemingly mingled trivial rhymes. As he would later with the riddles of Taliesin, so now with nursery tales, which in "To E. M.—A Ballad Of Nursery Rhyme," he traces back to the shepherd boy Tom whose primitive tales were polished and emended by his sister Kate (74–75).

Though he would fall under the influence of philosophers and philosophic systems from Rivers to Riding, his constant guide was what had been packed in the salt of time and tradition and came to him with his mother's milk: an English (though willful) poetic tradition and a respect for the basic demands of family, country, and god(dess).

"Country At War," a consciously Georgian poem, evokes deeper and more complex emotions than is usually true of Graves's war poems. The poem begins as a soldier in France asks: "And what of home—how goes it boys, / While we die here in stench and noise?" (CS 94). The reply to this predictable question is specific and begins and ends in the nursery, where children play, while outside there is a world of wildflowers and unripe pears as autumn comes. Graves does not need to add "under an English sky," in the manner of Brooke. The little England of the Georgians is clear and predictable, but the ending of the poem troubles as he equates the soldiers who "kill and kill again" with small boys who have committed some indiscretion: "Each cries for God to understand, / 'I could not help it, it was my hand.'" (95). With what is probably a reference to Lear's "like flies to wanton boys, they kill us for their sport," he looks for the causes of his troubles in the will of his gods.

Graves sees violence as integral to human beings and strongly indicates that not only does he regard the will to violence as stronger than human resolve, but he places awareness of the condition in childhood. This poem, though, is shocking because of the contrast between the idealized childhood of summer play that is refocused into anger intensive enough to make the child a killer, a view Graves might not have recognized had he not fought in the Great War. Reflecting on Charterhouse, Graves acknowledged the cruelty of his classmates and his own capacity for violence, but even in *Good-Bye To All That*, he did not equate them with the violence of war. The violence of the playing field was all but dismissed as a rite of passage, albeit one in which Graves took part even less than he did in the regimental mess. Probably he was kept from equating violence at Charterhouse with violence in battle by his own ties to a little England. And he would have regarded hazing and boxing matches as part of that rite of passage, called the public school.

The throes of marriage and parenthood did not make Graves more readily accommodate his present life to that ideal past. He did, though, continue his practice of escapist verse, as in "The Land of Whipperginny":

> Come closer yet, sweet honeysuckle, my coney, O my Jinny.
>   With a low sun gilding the bloom of the wood,
> Be this Heaven, be it Hell, or the Land of Whipperginny,
>   It lies in a fairy lustre, it savours most good. (*Whipperginny* 17)

The poem begins as a source of amusement and delight for his daughter Jenny but quickly reveals the reason for the source Graves gave between title and poem: "('Heaven or Hell or Whipperginny.'—Nashe's *Jack Wilton*)." Jack Wilton, Thomas Nashe's "unfortunate traveler," was a sometime mercenary. His description of a battle between the French and the "Switzers" must have reminded Graves of his own war, especially the Battle of the Somme:

> All the ground was strewed as thick with battle-axes as the carpenter's yard with chips: the plain appeared like a quagmire, overspread as it was with trampled dead bodies. In one place might you behold a heap of dead murdered men overwhelmed with a falling steed instead of a tombstone; in another place a bundle of bodies fettered together in their own bowels; and—as the tyrant Roman emperors used to tie condemned living caitiffs face to face to dead corpses—so were the half-living here mixed with squeezed carcasses long putrefied. And man might give arms that was an actor in that battle; for there were more arms and legs scattered in the field that day than will be gathered up till doomsday. (208–209)

In his next campaign, with Anabaptists led by John Leyden against the Emperor and the Duke of Saxony, he was with men poorly trained and armed who nevertheless were convinced they knew "as much of God's mind as richer men." Shortly before he decided to "cashier the new vocation of cavaliership" (216), he reflected on the beliefs (which took the place of common sense) of his comrades:

> Why, inspiration was their ordinary familiar, and buzzed in their ears like a bee in a box every hour what news from heaven, hell, and the land of whipperginnie. (210)

Without doubt, Jack Wilton is a soldier Graves could understand, and not simply because of their like experiences with the slaughter of battle and the duplicity of those who conduct wars. Nashe's choice of buzzing as metaphor would have echoed for Graves his own inner sound, which was growing in resonance and attribution: love as well as death, home as well as the battlefield. At this time in Graves's life, no experience was single, and nastiness or trauma could enter at any time. And as was true for Wilton's Anabaptists, so for Graves: inspiration did not have a clear source, not one he would openly admit. And his readers are left to wonder whether god or devil speaks through him—or mere nonsense. Surely Nashe recognized the problem, having expressed so well the confusion and despair that accompanies continued violence. Though working for a coherent answer, or image, Graves had not yet been able to accept such. Opposites, at times paradoxical ones, inform his poetry.

Though the second stanza of "The Land of Whipperginny" was inappropriate for his "sweet honeysuckle" (then age six), the poem does not seem to have been written for her but instead about the unease in a parent's mind as he reflects on the life he has helped into existence. Still ridden by the death he saw and barely escaped, Graves cannot write unwaveringly of a happy land, nor can he accept full responsibility for bringing children into a world where violence so quickly dismisses comfort and joy.

He somewhat assuages that guilt in the brooding "The Children of Darkness," (*Whipperginny*) in which he attributes the procreative drive to the desire of children to be born, not to the desire of the parents for the erotic or to see themselves writ small. In his early paper on hysteria, Freud asserted that sexual abuse was the primary cause of hysteria. Meeting a cool reception from his peers, he then placed the blame on the child and christened the now familiar Oedipus complex (Jones 166–169). In an oddly predictable manner, Graves, in the final version of the poem, places the responsibility for conception on the child rather than on parents who "shrank" from intimacy. That the child lives to be born is not the responsibility of the parents either, for only the resonance of the night drove them to sex. The parents in this published draft seem more sinned against than sinning.

Of the eleven extant drafts of this poem only what I assume to be the last three (very similar) drafts have the title "The Children of Darkness," and only one earlier draft, titled "Error," closely resembles them. Except for what may well be the seed of the poem, the earlier drafts and titles are much darker and indicate that Graves was not only concerned with the meaning of marriage, but with the significance of life. Discarded titles for this poem are "Darkness and Birth," "The Dark Birth," "Suicide's Philosophy of Birth," and *Philosophy of Suicide.*" The first sign of the existence of the poem, Graves wrote in a clear hand, without strikeouts, on an otherwise blank sheet of paper:

> In dead of midnight their caress
> Mixed us together, one from two—

Absent is the despair, easily termed existential, of the drafts that lead to the final version. In his accustomed manner, Graves would find the poem within his drafts. First creating a matrix, he would then find the form. The first eight drafts continue the tenderness of the two-line beginning, with such lines as "So in her warm dark we together flew" and "In warmth of midnight we together ~~drew~~ flew." No version of the poem continues with the tenderness of the opening, and all traces of it become lustful rather than tender.

Even the early drafts that contain the "warmth" are at odds with the tone. They are foreboding, speaking of the embryo's regret at being conceived and then being forced into the light. The poem comes close to its final form even in the early drafts, with Graves's revisions being largely concerned with ensuring that the emotional values of the words are consistent. He worked to eliminate all words except those connoting regret or anguish. Only in the fifth draft did he eliminate what had been the closing line of the poem: "In friendly darkness roars unstifled yet." The sound of a roar Graves will use again, as he has and will again use other loud sounds to signify intense experience, whether traumatic or not. Two other lines he wisely tried only in one early draft:

> Death, ~~loving willing~~ eager to pretend
> Himself my servant in the land of spears,

Graves did not easily shed Victorian poetic language. In the six early drafts, Graves only questions the opening line in the last: "We pricked them to embrace." By nature a prig, as he admitted, the pun on "pricked" would not likely remain. Besides, it introduces an element of wit alien to the poem. He did well to stay with "spurred," which he substituted in the sixth draft.

I assume this to be the final draft of the early version:

> We pricked them to embrace,
> And they each other knew,

So in her warm dark we together drew.
We changed to I, I of most ancient race
Then I, joy's child, knowing no discontent
With certitude about my business went;
Fancying means & use in that close place
Down to the light I grew
But light proved error; soul's regret
For friendly darkness roars unstifled yet.

The early drafts have only the one persona, that of the embryo. The introduction of a second persona, one who reflects on the embryo's existence,
changes neither the darkness of the poem nor the despair of the narrator.
But in adding the second persona, Graves takes the poem out of the terror
of the child approaching life to provide an expiation for the parent who
brings a child into such a world.

The draft with the title "Error" is a bridge between the earlier, darker
drafts, and the final ones, as shown in the last six lines:

O, is light, Error, that regret
for darkness roars unstifled yet,
That in this freedom, by faith won,
Only acts of doubt are done,
That unveiled eyes with tears are wet—
They loathe to gaze upon the Sun?

In later drafts, Graves would avoid such expository statements as he made
in "Error" and rely on image and narration, very much a technique of his
time and part of his poetic, increasingly informed by association, not reasoned statement. The changes he made in the three drafts which follow
this one are minor.

In the early versions, Graves withdrew again to childhood, seeking sanctuary from the trauma of adulthood. As in the nursery poems, he did not
find peace of mind. Instead, what frightened him in the outer world echoes
in his sanctuary. Recalling the poem "I Hate The Moon," we can easily
imagine soldiers drawing back into the protection of the darkness, knowing that they will be forced into the light. Even the "roaring darkness" is
preferable to being in the light, which leaves them no place to hide. That
the darkness is "roaring" yet safe indicates the degree to which Graves's
(or anyone's) ordinary understanding of a sanctuary has changed.

Of greater import, though, is Graves's despair with life itself. Recalled again is Eliot's "Love Song of J. Alfred Prufrock," written in 1917, which ends with a similarly despairing stanza:

We have lingered in the chambers of the sea
By sea-girls wreathed with seaweed red and brown
Till human voices wake us and we drown. (7)

Graves's "Children of Darkness," especially when its drafts are considered, is close to Eliot's in thought and image. Yet Graves's has not been associated with such terms as angst or existentialism. His English heritage, socially and poetically, has distracted readers from the intense anguish of his spiritual search.

A world of sound has replaced the predictable quietness in the poems of Keats he carried in his pocket during the war. The poems he wrote on the blank pages of that volume are made horrifying rather than ironic by their context. Keats's beautiful lady was awful, inspiring despair and terror in all: "and no birds sing." Though this passage could describe the aftermath of a battle, normal human referents are still present, not reversed as they were in Graves's war. Such disorientation as Graves and his comrades experienced made whatever remained of the normal past desirable. As did so many others, Graves would find that marriage and the family as they had been for his parents were not possible. Understandably, thoughts of death and suicide would occur as he watched, and participated in, the creation of new life. Such connections would not be made in a reasonable and predictable mind, but Graves was recording the accumulation of the irrational, of associations. To understand his poetic, we must move from manifest to hidden meanings. In "Children of Darkness," we move from pity to terror, increased by the nagging thought that Graves may have been contemplating his own suicide, a continuing concern in his poems, and perhaps in his life. Though Nancy Nicholson probably had the responsibility for his health and safety, he publicly credited his own poetry with saving him. Poetry does, in fact, not only save Graves but creates him—at least his spiritual life.

The war had closed the door on the Victorian age and opened on another one, first called Georgian and then Modernist. Robert Graves grew through each, shedding some traits as he adopted others. Whatever the appellation, basic to all is the power of association, usually to overcome quiet and reason. In *Whipperginny* at least, Graves has checked the intensity of dreams, writing as Rivers had said a poet must, by giving the dreams shape through image, character, and plot. Yet

Graves's psyche then contained experiences as terrifying as any of those in Mametz Wood.

Unable to dismiss the war from his poetry, he found himself led by such memories to the nursery, another occasion for primitive thought. The cause-and-effect world of his parents' reality, of the reality to which Aristotle had given narrative form, had scant control in either the trenches or the nursery. But the terrors of childhood had not overwhelmed him or put his sanity at risk. The reality of childhood—and its nightmares—belong to a traditional reality, expected and acceptable. Such reality found, for Graves, expression in dreams of "deeper sleep," as he discussed in *The Meaning of Dreams*. Such dreams are unlike the daytime reality of adults and often "go in the way that young children think and talk." Underlying such dreams is a terror which can be the source of madness, for Graves asserts that the "worst cases in the madhouse are those in which the patient is in such a deep sleep that nobody can make any sense of his utterances."

Yet Graves believed that a study of the dreams could lead to a cure, even of cases that had seemed hopeless. In fact, he was so convinced of the importance of dream therapy that he said, "Shakespeare's lines about the 'tale told by an idiot full of sound and fury, signifying nothing' are no longer justified" (*Meaning of Dreams* 34). But Graves knew well the tales that verge on madness. Probably he hoped that Rivers's view was right: that giving narrative form to the latent meanings of dreams would, ultimately, allow the dreamer to be rid of them, cured since the cause of the disturbance was no longer present. Thus the disturbance would disappear. With the war over, the violent dreams would cease. Yet I doubt that either was convinced. For Graves, madness provided a view of reality that was even more terrifying than mechanized war, a reality in which terror and chaos struggled with survival. Graves found a way for madness to sustain life.

For Graves to use childhood experiences as analogies for the war is his way of relating two forms of reality that differ so greatly from what he termed "logically-tuned" tales, those that tell of the accepted reality of adulthood (*Meaning of Dreams* 34). Graves found form as well as content in his disturbance. Predictably, he found a touchstone for his own tales in the writings of Lewis Carroll, as we see in "Alice," the first poem in *Welchman's Hose*. Graves's Alice is a child who escapes the "[d]ull round of mid-Victorian routine," much as had Graves, by the chance discovery of a land beyond the glass. There existed neither "Victoria's golden rule" nor "formal logic." Instead, there began "that lubberland of dream and laughter."

There Apuleius "pastured his Golden Ass" and "young Gargantua made full holiday" (*Welchman's Hose* 2). When he wrote this poem, the images were not simply escapist but were part of the effect of shell shock. A part of his childhood, *Alice in Wonderland* acquired new value for Graves, who had found all understanding of beliefs turned topsy-turvy by the war in France. Patriotism was meaningless, as was survival in the world of the emotionally wounded. Yet he knew that, though disturbed, he had to act as if he shared the reality of others, which must have been extremely difficult after he saw the "death-white Fay" of "A History." Yet as his daughter, Catherine Dalton, wrote to me, he would have been thought mad if he had revealed his spiritual experience. So to tell of his reality, Graves resorted to structures of nursery tales, which presume a reality that adults no longer share. Little from childhood remained as it had been, with the notable exception of a book that said the reverse is always true. Graves's tacit acceptance of a distinction between Queen and Kitten seems, at first, at odds with the associative process of his poems, a process in which the battlefield recalled the nursery and opposites were united.

By 1925, when *Welchman's Hose* was published, Graves had stepped into the reality of the Goddess, or she into his, but he would write of this experience through the unexorcised war demons of his dreams. Other terrors had led him to awe: woman and power. In time, he would combine the two into one icon: the White Goddess. But not now. Now the woman would trouble his dreams, leading him into the terror of "deeper sleep." Graves had, in his obsessive writing about the violence of war, lifted pain "out of the ironclad privacy of the body into speech," in the words of Professor Scarry. And as she observed, once out of privacy it "immediately falls back in." The experience of pain resists language: "Its absolute claim for acknowledgement contributes to its being ultimately unacknowledged" (60–61). Pain, loss of control, and a reliance on these found expression for Graves in his devotion to a love he could accept but not explain, a love he experienced in the "unfamiliar imagery" of "A Valentine." The presence of pain then and forever dominated his writing.

The power of kings and warriors, though able to cause terror, seems to have become his familiar, the talisman leading him out of the psyche, allowing him to distinguish between queens and kittens. He would maintain the distinction in *Poems (1914–1926)*, his first collection. Graves used this volume to portray his poetic concerns at the time. He began the volume with "The Poet in the Nursery," which tells of his theft of a book from the library of an older poet, a book filled with wonderful sounds and phrases, with "splendid words a sentence long," and complicated meters and rhymes (3–4). What this poem expresses is the craft of the poet, not the terror and awe that people the unconscious, scarcely the tune Graves consistently played in his nursery poems. Almost predictably, Graves had echoed the views of Rivers, and his departure in "The Poet in the Nursery" is implied in Rivers's own discussion in *Conflict and Dream* of the poet and the dreamer. Rivers contended that one could study the "manifest content" of a poem and find how that content had been suggested by the experience of the poet. The content for Rivers was expressed through the images, which symbolically revealed the conflict in the poet's mind, thus revealing the "underlying meaning or latent content" of the poem, which was often quite different from the obvious expression of the "manifest content." By "condensation" the poet expresses many experiences through "a simple image" (148). Graves's early adherence to this method is evident, but his divergence from it is as obvious in the poems he selected for *Poems (1914–1926)*, a selection which illustrates Rivers's caveat in *Conflict and Dream* for not explaining the similarities he believed existed between dreaming and writing poetry. Not being a poet, Rivers could not give evidence of his theory. Instead, he expected such evidence of "the real mechanism of artistic production" to come "when poets and other artists have set to work to analyze the products of their artistry" (149).

As if lecturing Rivers, as well as his readers, Graves began *Poems (1914–1926)* with a poem about the maze of language, not of physical or psychological reality. Entranced by the beauty of an incomprehensible language, the young poet in the poem abandons his own narratives. Though he fell under the fortunate influence of others, Graves himself never abandoned his own reality. Instead, what he learned from others became his own property, bearing his signature.

Poems of mazes and webs continue in this collection, such as "Attercop: The All-Wise Spider." I would not stress these poems so much here if Graves had not chosen to close *Poems (1914–1926)* with one of his best-known poems, "The Cool Web." Long before the Confessional Poets preened their neuroses, Graves considered that the danger to the poet of losing touch with primitive terror and awe would be that poems would become academic. Yet if the poet does not "spell away" that reality, madness is inevitable. Having lived in the madness of war and its bruising aftermath, a deranged peace, Graves knew what to expect. Yet he almost seemed willing to run the risk. Almost but not quite. As Graves looked into the mazes, webs, and riddles of his culture, he would find their intent was not to diminish awe but to allow only the deserving to experience it.

When I met Robert Graves in his study, he showed me strands of his web, though I could recognize few:

"Do you know who sheared the sheep, spun the wool, and wove
    the rug?"
"Do you know what the inscription on this ring says?"
"Do you know why I have this dagger?"

With Robert Graves dead, I search as I think he would have wished me to: in the intricacies of his work. Such intricacies reveal the complexity of the seemingly simple lives of children and the seemingly simple love of a father for a child. The neuroses of the shell-shocked soldier opened a door into the awe and terror of Graves's inner world, the world of his poetry, and that opened door led to the nursery before it led to the bedroom.

What Rivers termed "manifest" meaning in Graves's poems about childhood and children is clearly evident in the subject matter: his remembrances of his own childhood and his comments on the lives of his children with some attention to clearly made-up ones. But the "hidden" meaning that both Rivers and Graves were concerned with is a different matter altogether. In the poems he wrote during the war and after, he tried to establish a continuum that began in his own childhood, whose traumas he survived, and continued through battle, whose traumas he hoped to survive. He could not, however, easily escape the terror of battle, and in these poems never does he introduce the saving grace of paradox that he would find only in the passionate love of a woman. The poems of childhood maintain touch with tender emotions as well as frightening ones, but seldom is he able to make the two mesh, as he would in "To Juan at the Winter Solstice" (CP 2:150–151). In a poem for his son, Juan, Graves was willing to write of the awe and terror of his love for a woman and a goddess. But by then he knew the love of women and had left his own nursery memories behind. They departed slowly, having been necessary for the soldier's survival. But with the birth of his own children and his slow accommodation of the lasting effects of war neurosis, Graves's poems moved beyond the nursery and into the marriage bed. There he again found terror and awe, and in the feminine, a stronger support than he had during the childhood he survived. In writing that life, he moved away from the late-Victorian world of his mentor, Edward Marsh, and into the world of the Modernists, though without accepting their poetic. He remained staunchly English even in exile.

CHAPTER 5

THE LOVER

A Valentine

The hunter to the husbandman
Pays tribute since our love began,
And to love-loyalty dedicates
The phantom kills he meditates.
Let me embrace, embracing you,
Beauty of other shape and hue,
Odd glinting graces of which none
Shone more than candle to your sun,
Your well-kissed hand was beckoning me
In unfamiliar imagery—
Smile your forgiveness; each bright ghost
Dives in love's glory and is lost,
Yielding your comprehensive pride
A homage, even to suicide.

Whipperginny

Robert Graves's loves and love life have preoccupied his biographers often to the exclusion of his poems—the reason we all have for writing about his love life. The bare bones of this fabled love life are: the twig was bent by an overbearing mother; in a single-sex public school he fell in love (a sexless love, he claimed) with a younger boy who later proved to be homosexual; in the army he remained a virgin although surrounded by license; he married a woman as naive as himself, and they had four children; then all was changed, utterly changed, by the arrival of Laura Riding, who dominated him; when she married, he did as well. Later muses in the form of young women provided a medium for his worship of the White Goddess, whom he implied he discovered while writing *The Golden Fleece* in 1943.

This is all true except that Laura Riding did not create the love-ridden poet, and the muses were more numerous than the four claimed by his biographers. His experience of the Goddess at least as early as 1924 is of greater significance than either Riding or the number of muses spinning in the head of the poet.

What is clear from Graves's earliest love poems is that, being a bit of a prig, he was dominated by a desire he could only accept if it were cloaked in obsessions other than the physically erotic. As "Oh, and Oh," an early poem from *Over the Brazier* shows, Graves was likely to swoon at the thought of his beloved but was made very uncomfortable by mundane and unavoidable comparisons as he looked at hoi polloi, who "Craw and kiss and cuddle" in open doorways. He found the love of louts and sluts to be "loathsome," an "unbelievable ugliness" (16). Almost ten years later, in *The Waste Land*, T. S. Eliot would echo Graves's revulsion with the sexual life of hoi polloi, but he wasn't a soldier risking his life daily. In "Oh, and Oh," Graves strikes out at his opponents with a quite bourgeois vengeance. Graves quite openly referred to himself as bourgeois in letters to March and Sassoon, and in a letter to Sassoon on 13 January 1919, Graves wrote jovially of the fate of the bourgeoisie:

> But I think that despite Lloyd George, Clemenceau & the Capitalists we can save Western Europe from so deep an operation and at any rate have the bourgeoises alive: being a bourgeois myself I want to remain alive. (BCNYPL)

To think of Graves with the advantage of knowing about his whole life and writing does not lead inevitably to call him "bourgeois." But he was of his time and class: easily offended, well-schooled, and well-drilled in a Victorian morality, and from a family that would have been considered culturally bourgeois at the time. Politically, he would have distanced himself from any leftist attitude and would have welcomed their disapproval of the bourgeoisie, a disapproval based on Marx's view of the ideology of capitalists as antithetical to that of the proletariat. Graves never significantly changed his politics. Though well placed in literary circles, his father was a civil servant; though financially stable, his parents clearly were not landed gentry. In his poems he held to his English identity and to his class.

Though Graves wrote explicitly of the erotic in his poetry, as did his early idol Rupert Brooke, he did not break completely from his bourgeois manner. Graves's loss of virginity informed his poetry with details and resonances that appeared neither in his correspondence nor in his conversations—as much as we know of the latter seems to reflect his prudishness. But the poems are alive with sexuality.

To accept Graves's assertion that he did not have a physical relationship with the boy at Charterhouse is the simplest answer to several problems, the main one being the difference between the love poems he wrote the boy and those he wrote Nancy, his wife. The similarities are clear: he is obsessive, and he needs to gild the lily. Though the poems to the boy are watery Victorian love poems (what Graves himself might call "wet"), the poems to Nancy contain specific physical images, as in "The Kiss," which he published in *The Treasure Box* (1919). Still half in love with convenient poetic language, Graves overcame his Georgian leanings to give love a physical trait, a sound that stuns and numbs, that devastates and obliterates meaning and even the desire to live. Graves's attempts to distinguish between "Love," "Passion," and "Death" are unconvincing, hence unsuccessful. But we must remember that his courtier-like love for the boy at Charterhouse had not been tested in the body. The love Graves describes in "The Kiss" had been so tested, and Graves had found postcoital love to be devastating, the emptiness filled with dread of a loss that might be permanent, a view of Graves and this poem echoed by the critic Patrick Quinn (54). After all, he had made his wife sole proprietor of their love. She was host, with all the obligations to heal her wounded lover.

Graves would reprint "The Kiss" in 1921 in *The Pier-Glass;* but before that, the poems in *Country Sentiment* (1920) gave the terms and values of the love he shared with Nancy Nicholson, to whom he dedicated both volumes. She did not take his surname when they married and insisted their daughters be given the name Nicholson. She was clearly dominant in the marriage, giving him impossible tasks, which like a dutiful and loving knight he accomplished. When she had an ideal cottage in mind, he found "World's End," a prophetic name since there Graves would bury the last remnant of his Victorian attire, patriarchal dominance.

He does not bother with disguise in his ballad-like poem "Neglectful Edward," which is about a man who brings to a woman named Nancy all that he can yet still is reprimanded. The woman is not likely to have been named Nancy by chance. Here, Graves continues the analogy method that had been successful for him and stays in the genre of nursery rhymes, though the analogy is buried rather than explicit. He did not provide clues to the source of poems written about love as he had for the poems about war. The poems about the trauma of love were as close to the experience as he could get, for poetry was and would remain the most accurate way he had of recording his spiritual life. And that life was based in the trauma of love. In a letter to Edward Marsh on 13 January 1919, Graves was confident in the lasting value of poems he called "the Nursery Rhymes," such as "Henry Was a Worthy King" and "Careless Lady." "Neglectful Edward" is another poem in which he tells of heart deep troubles in "Nursery Rhymes." Graves emerges in *Country Sentiment* as obsessively dutiful and subservient but unable to distance the trauma, what Rivers would have called the "hidden meaning," of the poems.

Though still haunted by memories of war, he found passion and love growing in significance. Constantly present is his dependence on the woman, in this case Nancy, as in "Song: One Hard Look," that poem of small events in *Country Sentiment*. That these are largely domestic indicates that all was not beer and skittles in the household. The irritation with a child occurs for everyone, as do quarrels between husband and wife, but few would view a smile as "deadly" or a frown as able to end love. These verses string together not so much similar experiences but instead experiences that produce similar effects, ones making Graves fear for life and sanity. For him, at this time, whether smiling or frowning, love was traumatic. This trauma was a condition he would not only learn to live with, but one that would lead him ever deeper into personal and cultural mysteries.

The Pier-Glass (1921), also dedicated to Nancy Nicholson, further develops the personae of lovers established in *Country Sentiment*. "The Troll's Nosegay" seems, at first, a reiteration of the displeased woman and the obsequious lover. Since the lady demands flowers out of season, the troll conjures up a bouquet of "Cold fog-drawn Lily, pale mist-magic Rose" and "elvish unsubstantial Mignonette," but finds the demanding lady unwilling to respond at all. She remains mysterious, indecipherable for him. He can but accept her whims, her decisions, without presuming to understand (13). The lady from this nursery poem will change in name in Graves's poetry, but she will remain, and he will never presume to understand her.

The Victorian trappings of knights and ladies are recalled here; but the poet has lost earlier prestige and has become a troll, usually the butt of jokes. Graves was consciously changing his poetic and predicted in a letter to Marsh on 7 October 1920 that *The Pier-Glass* might not find general approval: "people may dislike these but, as coming from R. G. who has a reputation principally based on nursery rhymes" (BCNYPL). Marsh was among those who did not like the new poems, which deviated from linear and rational thinking. Marsh wanted a clear plot, unambiguous statements, distinct genres, and a poetic persona as close to Rupert Brooke's as possible. When Graves moved beyond physical truth and into spiritual reality, his poetry was no longer directed by the rhetoric of a rational causality, which Marsh and the Georgians expected. Nothing was as important for Graves as expressing that spiritual reality—not the dignity of the poet, the clarity of statement, or the purity of genre.

The diminution of Graves's sense of self would continue and intensify. He writes from the same perspective as did Keats in "La Belle Dame Sans Merci," an important poem for Graves because, as he read it, the poem equated the effects of love and death, as he so often did. Discussing "La Belle Dame Sans Merci" in *On English Poetry* (1922), Graves deliberately employed "History and psychology" in the service of literary interpretation, presenting himself as quite modern and scientific, holding onto reasoned patterns of behavior even as experience itself belies what his reason tells him. But in whatever persona he writes, Graves presents death and love in the same images and metaphors. The reason for such equation appears to be that in both cases Graves found himself in the willing control of others. Neither the continuance of life or love was of his choosing.

"The Pier-Glass," titular for the volume, is again in first person. As he has frequently in earlier poems, in this one the poet assumes a feminine role, resonant of Tennyson's "Lady of Shalott" and resembling the Lady in that both poets identify with women driven to distraction and death, island dwellers cursed never to look at life directly, never to be happily involved:

> Face about
> Peer rather in the glass once more, take note
> Of self, the grey lips and long hair disheveled,
> Sleep-staring eyes. Ah, mirror, for Christ's love
> Give me one token that there still abides
> Remote, beyond this island mystery
> So be it only this side hope, somewhere,
> In streams, on sun-warm mountain pasturage,
> True life, natural breath, not this phantasm. (15)

Like Tennyson in "The Lady of Shalott," Graves identifies poetic talent as feminine, but Graves's woman is not frail and defenseless. Instead, she has held life in her hand:

> Did not my answer please the Master's ear?
> Yet, I'll stay obstinate. How went the question,
> A paltry question set on the elements

Of love and the wronged lover's obligation;
Kill or forgive? Still does the bed ooze blood?
Let it drip down till every floor-plank rot!
Yet shall I answer, challenging the judgement—
"Kill, strike the blow again, spite what come."
"Kill, strike, again, again," the bees in chorus hum. (16)

The bees and their inescapable buzzing, identified earlier in the poem as "bee-sergeants" in the service of their "queen," again unite the traumas of war and love. The image of sound this time is identified closely with the subservience of the male to a superior, whether a superior officer or a queen. The reversal of power suggests that Graves was reflecting on Tennyson's poem, not being "parasitical" of Tennyson, as Donald Davie asserted (41).

Graves reprinted the complete poem, including the last section in which the ghost relives the murder, in *Poems (1914–1926)*, but his *Collected Poems* (1938) omits the last section. The poem is still haunting but not violent since Graves lessened the resonance of trauma caused both by war and love. Curiously, as he grows closer to admitting the existence of the White Goddess, he is less likely to present the force of her reality. Perhaps he wanted to cut ties with knowledge that had come to him through the means of psychological analyses, or, and this seems more likely, he wanted to lessen the revelation of his own powerful experiences in poems that had their origins in the frightening reality of his spirit and in the psychological bruising of his early traumas. The change in the revision of the poem is away from the violent, blood-thirsty woman who haunts the house staring succubus-like from mirrors. He is, without doubt, moving away from an identity Martin Seymour-Smith saw as directed by war neurosis though, like the woman narrator, Graves is "haunted by guilt" and lives in a "phantasm" (92). For Seymour-Smith, the trauma of shell shock revealed Graves's *general* neurasthenia or neuroses. Graves would more likely have said that the neurasthenia led him to the reality of the unconscious; there dream and association replaced the reason and predictability of Aristotle's reality. Having become aware of the life of the unconscious, Graves next became aware of the power of the feminine, which enabled him to prefigure the dominant metaphor of the last half of his life: the White Goddess. Carl Jung would have said that Graves had met his archetypes. Such a view answers much, though neglects Graves's own early ambiguity with the role of women. He identified with their helplessness in Victorian England. As a soldier he lost control of life and spirit as they did as women, and his wife Nancy constantly iterated that the wrongs done to him and others in the war scarcely compared with the mistreatment of women historically. Yet his own experience of women was of beings more powerful than he: his mother and his wife. Seymour-Smith's view of the poem, however, must be given its due: Nancy was a scatterbrain whose quirks dominated his life, for though he had ceased to love her, he recognized the right dominance of woman, the power of the matriarchy. So he created the homicidal succubus of "The Pier-Glass" as a forceful substitute for Nancy (94). Such a view is only half convincing, the half about his acceptance of the matriarchy and the power of woman. Nancy wielded the power, and he would have stayed with her if he could.

Quite possibly the face that looks from the mirror prefigures the "death-white Fay" he will soon present in "A History," the Goddess herself. But the descriptions are not close, suggesting that the face in the mirror is Graves's muse, not the Goddess herself: the compelling and frightening face of death. The face of battle has become the face of his muse, his own creative self.

Though memories of the war still preoccupy him, Graves's hauntings at this time are largely of his new understanding of love and the nature of woman. In "Catherine Drury," familiar themes appear as a mother and daughter talk of Edward, the mother's disaffected lover, and his new lover, Catherine Drury:

> Edward's heart will melt away,
>   His head go buzz,
> And if he thinks you read his mind,
> Better you had been struck stone blind. (TB 29)

The sound of passion and buzz of the gnat here become equated with the sound of violence, as in "The Gnat," which was also first published in *The Pier-Glass*. In this poem, though, Edward is the male of the Victorian household, violent and domineering except possibly in the presence of Catherine Drury. She has drawn him away from wife and hearth, the passionate and dark other woman. Such a triangle would often people Graves's writings and, clearly, preoccupied him. The model though is, most likely, not the typical ménage à trois that would develop with the arrival of Laura Riding, but one in which the third party is very decidedly the other, a spiritual rather than a physical being. She lies behind the poems of deceit and betrayal, suggesting that she is the one betrayed. Graves, just as much as Tennyson, is troubled that being of the world will kill his gift. The isolated village of Deya on the island of Mallorca would become his sanctuary when he left England with Riding in 1929. The choice was not only fortuitous but, on many levels, necessary.

As often identifying with the social inferiority of the woman as attesting to her power, Graves is less concerned with societal wrongs than with the power of passion and love, noting in "Blackhorse Lane" that love came unexpectedly "one blue windy morning," leaving the lovers breathless and unable to know whether they felt joy or pain (PG 52). Love here, as always, for Graves is not single and uncomplicated. It is paradoxical and so must be accepted or rejected, but not understood in terms of reason or even common sense. Reasonably, and emotionally, opposites should not coexist: but pain be pain, pleasure be pleasure. However, in the spiritual and creative life of Graves, the two combine as the terms of his existence and his writing, and he must give himself up to what he cannot understand, to a power that will not explain itself.

Whether in the persona of man or woman, Graves prefers to portray the woman as more powerful emotionally than the man. When more powerful, the man is in the patriarchal role of soldier, someone who seduces or rapes. But the woman can, for Graves, heal or destroy by her very self, usually without gun or knife, as he shows in "A Valentine," which is preface to *Whipperginny* (1923). Here Graves ascribes to love, or, more accurately, to a woman the power, right, and authority to determine not only his health but his life or death. By considering "suicide" an "homage" to the woman, he not only places a barely comprehensible burden on her, but reveals as well a mind too troubled to be called sane. That his understanding is guided by terms that cannot accommodate reason is evident in "Author's Note" to *Whipperginny*. Here he describes the poetry in *Country Sentiment* and *The Pier-Glass* as expressing his "desire to escape from a painful war neurosis into an Arcadia of amatory fancy" (v). Arcadia had not been, however, inhabited by homicidal succubi and incubi as were the poems in *Country Sentiment* and *The Pier-Glass*. That he can consider such poetry "amatory fancy" indicates the severity of what he considered his "war neurosis" if, indeed, the diagnosis "neurotic" has validity in this situation. Neurotic, then, could extend to delusion, and Graves was delusional only if he did *not actually see* these powerful spiritual beings.

Equally troubling in "Author's Note" is Graves's claim that the poems in *Whipperginny* are "of less emotional intensity" than the ones in preceding volumes. "A Valentine," in which Graves offers his heart, literally, is more emotionally intense and troubled than anything he had published before. This is his love poem to Keats's "La Belle Dame Sans Merci," a poem Graves considered part of the "familiar furniture" of his mind. In his final remark in "Author's Note," Graves dismisses any responsibility to provide vicarious emotional experiences for his readers, and he is both blunt and vulgar in doing so, which in my reading of him is unique:

> I have no apology to offer, but only this proverb from the Chinese, that *the petulant protests of all the lords and ladies of the Imperial Court will weigh little with the whale when, recovering from his painful excretory condition, he need no longer supply the Guild of Honorable Perfumers with their accustomed weight of ambergris.* (vi)

The poems that follow "Author's Note" evidence his hauntings more than any except, possibly, "The Pier-Glass." None of his ghosts has been exorcised, and love has led him close to suicide.

Basically, there are three explanations for Graves's poems of love and violence, his poems of hauntings:

1. The phantasmal are rhetorical, extensions of his earlier analogies, a means to express the complex through condensation. As such, they would resemble Jung's archetypes.

2. He had transferred to his wife all control. She had become the power that had been the war, and was to make him believe he could survive any irrationality, any violence.

3. He had actually experienced the spiritual power he called the Goddess.

The first explanation seems empty since he consciously abandoned the rhetorical model of the analogy and the evidence provided by psychoanalysis. If either or both of the other two are true, Graves had moved into a reality most people will only know in moments of great passion or fear, moments of vulnerability and acceptance.

Such does not seem to have been the everyday life of Nicholson and Graves. Living at Boar's Hill, Oxford, in a cottage rented from the Masefields, Robert and Nancy began a life that should have been idyllic. They were young and in love, with access to the most significant writers of their time. They knew Edmund Gosse, visited with Thomas Hardy, saw the Masefields regularly. The young poets, such as T. S. Eliot, were close by. They had the William Nicholsons for steady company, a most contemporary and fashionable gathering. Soon Graves would be published by the eminent Woolfs. But as the poem "Sullen Moods" in *Whipperginny* shows, all was not easy in the household. Tracing the development of this poem from first draft to published version indicates the tenuousness of Graves's emotional stability and his growing reliance on Nancy, both as his lover and as his spiritual mentor.

Love, do not count your labour lost
Though I turn sullen, grim, retired
Even at your side; my thought is crossed
With fancies by old longings fired.

And when I answer you, some days
Vaguely and wildly, do not fear
That my love walks forbidden ways,
Breaking the ties that hold it here.

If I speak gruffly, this mood is
Mere indignation at my own
Shortcomings, plagues, uncertainties;
I forget the gentler tone.

You, now that you have come to be
My one beginning, prime and end,
I count at last as wholly me,
Lover no longer nor yet friend.

Friendship is flattery, though close hid;
Must I then flatter my own mind?
And must (which laws of shame forbid)
Blind love of you make self-love blind?

Do not repay me my own coin,
The sharp rebuke, the frown, the groan;
Remind me, rather to disjoin
Your emanation from my own.

Graves wrote "Sullen Moods" in the spring of 1921 when he and Nancy Nicholson were living at Boar's Hill in Oxford, where they also ran a shop to provide household supplies. The undertaking was a financial failure and, at first glance, seems to have been a most unnecessary distraction for Graves, who found himself drawn into the role of shopkeeper, as well as children's nurse, when Nancy was not well. Such is the view held by Graves's biographers. His daughter, Catherine Dalton, considers the "return" of her father's "shell shock" and the necessity of her mother's nursing him as the causes of the shop's closing. The distractions and irritations were many, understandably causing tensions and, clearly, unpleasant moods. In "Sullen Moods" he apologizes for his unpleasantness, but this seemingly simple poem had much more complex concerns. The drafts of the poem reveal that Graves had very much placed himself under the control of his wife, so much so that in "A Valentine," which also first appeared in *Whipperginny*, he offered his suicide as homage. He would offer the White Goddess no more. In the poems in *Country Sentiment* and *The Pier-Glass*, Graves tells of the healing power of his wife's love as he recovered from the effects of World War I. Graves's beloved takes command of his body and spirit to heal, not destroy, him.

What seems to be the first draft of "Sullen Moods" was written on an envelope with these words:

> *Oxford Times*
> 11 rooms
> Nice Gardens
> Every Convenience
> *For Sale*

Clearly, Nancy had already set him the task of finding a new place to live, and she knew exactly what she wanted. Graves may well have been writing out of irritation when he put the first words of "Sullen Moods" on the envelope:

> Self-love with love of you betwined
> And must which laws of shame forbid

These two phrases will essentially inform all drafts of the poem: Graves cannot separate love of himself from love of his wife and is bound by laws other than those of marriage vows. Self-love, as Graves uses the phrase, is *amour propre*, one's own self-respect. In Graves's case, he can make no separation between his love for his wife and his own sense of worth. "Betwined" perhaps, but without doubt his self-love is dependent on her acceptance.

I assume the drafts to be earliest which are brief, incomplete, and with extensive strikeouts. There are three such drafts, which may well have been written in the order of my discussion. The first is very rough with more words stricken than not. Several clauses, though, emerge as "Help me see you as before"; "When overwhelmed ~~and dazed~~ and almost [unreadable] I stumbled on that ~~hidden~~ secret door ~~that separates~~ which saves the ~~living man~~ from the ghost." Graves's concern with the world of the living and the world of the ghost is repeated in many poems at this time, reflecting his own inquiry into the nature of the unconscious. He wrote repeatedly in *The Meaning of Dreams, On English Poetry,* and *Poetic Unreason* of the similarity of dreaming and writing poetry, both concerned with conflict. The difference seemed to be that the poet (Graves) did not want to resolve the conflict but to use it as a doorway into the unconscious, much as would a psychologist working with a patient's dreams.

The verso of this page has few strikeouts and is in a clearer hand: "~~Think; it no sign of~~"; "Never ~~Do not think that our believe that our faithful love is not lost~~"; "Forgive me, do not think all lost"; "Think it no warning of true love lost"; "Do not think our love is lost It is no sign of love half lost." In the published version, this page resulted in: "Love, do not count your labour lost," which is very different from Graves's pleading in the draft. He did well in this early draft to strike out "true love," though he did not immediately abandon the phrase. The differing versions reflect Graves's investigations into the "sub-personalities" of the poet. Or to be clearer: he was role-playing, as probably Nancy was as well. Quite likely, the role-playing and his dependence on Nancy were essential to his recovery from the trauma of war. In a letter dated 31 October 1997, Catherine Dalton wrote to me about this time in the life of the Graves family and mentioned her mother's "enormous care (and cure) of his neurasthenia." Graves extrapolated variously and well from his experience, constructing such love poems as "The Pier-Glass," "Incubus," and "Richard Roe and John Doe" from his married life. An early draft of "Sullen Moods" goes beyond extrapolation and role-playing into the abject fear of the poet that his slighting of his wife may cause her to leave him.

The next draft was written on the verso of a letter (dated 2 April 1921) from Holbrook Jackson, editor of *To-Day: A Journal of Literature and Ideas,* asking Graves for a poem to include in the June issue. Although there are numerous strikeouts and some unreadable words, the concern is clear: Graves believes their love is changing, perhaps into a kind of friendship:

> ~~But then~~ know that
> ~~But listen,~~ since you
> ~~Stoutheart you have come~~ came to be
> And hold ~~guard~~ my life at either both ends
> Thy whole life's care from start of end

I think of you as wholly [unreadable]
~~Of flattery due to common friends a mere~~ friend
~~No more a lover Lover~~ no longer nor ~~than~~ yet a friend
Friendship is flattery, who could ~~need~~ use
The flatterers art on ~~my~~ his mind will cause a worse abuse
Self love ~~is subject to is always discovers of~~ much mistrust deception
Than [unreadable] behind that laying
[unreadable]
do not hurt yourself from me
[unreadable]
And pay me back
I seldom think

Graves used two pens in this draft, suggesting he went back to it. One is very sharp and dark, the other lighter. The last two lines are in the clearer pen. This page provides an early draft for the last two stanzas and makes the connection between the two which Graves did not make when he published the poem: self-love results in the deception of flattery as a way of distancing people from each other; hence disguised moods are flattery (paying undue homage), which he will not do with her, accepting blame for his bad mood. He hopes she will be open with him, not pay him back with flattery. This reading differs from that of the published version, in which he simply asks that she not repeat his mood. Keeping the concern with flattery, Graves wrote, "Must I then flatter my own mind?" Lacking her love, his own self-love would be diminished to friendship, scarcely a condition to provide him with the will to live.

The next draft is on an opened envelope from the Bocardo Press, Oxford, dated 16 April 1921. The half with the address is almost unreadable, though the words "fear" and "alarm" are decipherable. The other half of the page begins:

His harshness is no proof of friendship lost
~~That~~ It grow sullen ~~and~~ and retire
Even in your presence my my
With fancies ~~that no thinking end~~
Or if by old fears crossed tired
~~And that~~ I answer you sometimes days
Vaguely and wildly so that you stand
That my love walks in other ways
Forgetting That it ~~home and children~~ what ~~once bound~~ me
        should bind here

Tired Grown! With scorn ~~all that binds~~ me for me
Sick For sweetheart long since came to be all
But you have ~~become~~
So ~~intimate a part~~ of me
Essential Essentially to to me
And past the ~~flattery~~ of
Such flattery as I give my friends
~~Essential part of my~~ own

Graves does not enter new material in this draft, but seems to be trying out words, which he will largely, and wisely, reject: "Essential Essentially," "sweetheart" like "Stoutheart" in the previous draft were not retained in the published version. The word "fancies" will be echoed in "Author's Note" to *Whipperginny* indicating that "Sullen Moods" is one of those "amatory fancies" that helped his recovery from his war neurosis. "Sullen Moods" can be termed a fancy most easily if fancy is thought of as a distraction or illusion, though caprice may be closer to Graves's meaning.

The next draft has one strikeout, and in a clear hand gives the title and a few phrases:

Sullen Moods
It is no proof
Bound
Blind to the laws that hold it here
Denying
~~Despising~~ home and children
here

The title and the incomplete sentence appear on the page as if Graves intended a more formal draft of the poem, but he breaks off the draft. The rest of the page has only two irregularly spaced phrases. Graves may well be again testing words. But the irregular spacing of these phrases and the stricken out "Despising" suggest Graves fell into a deeper and darker mood soon after he began writing the draft. Whatever the case, his withdrawal from "home and children" is the concern of this draft. No more should be made of this, however, than would be of anyone's irritation.

In the next draft, he completes what he began with the above failed draft, a test version of the poem, close to what will be the published one:

True love
~~Kindness~~
It is no proof of ~~friendship~~ lost
That I grow sullen, grim, retired
Even in your presence, my mind crossed
With fancies by old longings fired,

Or-that I answer you some days
Vaguely and wildly, so you fear

That my love walks in alien ways
With scorn for what once bound it here.

~~When~~ If I speak harsh this harshness is
which ~~Sign of great fury~~ indignation with my own
Short comings, plagues, infirmities
And I forget to change my tone
For you who long ~~since came grown~~ proved to be
My ~~whole~~ one beginning, prime, and end.
I think of you as wholly me
Lover no longer nor yet friend

Friendship is flattery, who can who could use my his own
                his own mind?
The soothing art
The. laws of shame refuse
Self-love ~~would earn a worse abuse~~
~~That self mistrust, lagging behind~~
~~And you as~~
And love ~~for you is with self~~ entwined
~~How then~~ Your self with myself close
~~Then~~ do so do not pay me my coin,
With sharp reproof or ~~sullen~~ frown or groan,
But ~~let our your memories~~ my memory to disjoin
Your emanation from my own.

Become once more the distant light
The hope of glory not yet proved
Of a perfection wasted quite
Since by such imperfection loved.

Graves signed this draft as he did a very similar one. Most changes in the two drafts concern diction. Increasingly, he replaces the flat and prosy and the self-consciously poetic with words that reflect his own poetic language, a heightened poetic not yet free of the Georgian influence.

In these drafts, however, he wrote a final stanza that he did not retain in the published version:

> Be once again the distant light
> Promise of glory, not yet known
> In full perfection—wasted quite
> When on my imperfection thrown.

He retained this stanza in four of the last five drafts, eliminating it only from an incomplete draft. This final stanza is quite remarkable in anticipating what will be his relationship in the future with Woman/Muse/Goddess.

Four of these drafts begin:

> Think it no proof of love half-lost
> That I grow sullen, grim, retired
> Even in your presence, my mind crossed
> With fancies by old longings fired

And two of the drafts retain the stanza from a very early draft:

> Help me to see you as before
> When overwhelmed and dead almost
> I stumbled on that secret door
> Which saves the live man from the ghost.

This stanza was retained in what I assume was the final draft, which began as did the published version:

> Love, do not think count your labour lost
> Though I turn sullen, grim, retired
> Even at your side; my thought is crossed
> With fancies by old longings fired.

With the exception of the final stanza, this draft is essentially the same as the published one. Graves did well to eliminate the final stanza with its Victorian, even Tennysonian, resonance. He was at this time still struggling with his father's influence, an influence he credited Edward Marsh with having helped him overcome.

Aside from the final stanza, the most important part of these late drafts is a marginal comment Graves made on what is probably the next to last, since it retains the opening: "Think it no proof of love half-lost." At the bottom of the page, underneath his signature, Graves wrote in a very clear hand:

Proof of hypnotic
not being able to
remember
original
drafts

This statement indicates Graves's understanding of the poetic process as trancelike or dreamlike, a belief familiar to those more acquainted with Graves's later writings, those initiated by "The Roebuck in the Thicket," the inspired beginning of *The White Goddess*. Graves's "Postscript 1960" to *The White Goddess* explains that his awareness of the Goddess occurred while he was working on *The Golden Fleece*. He wrote about seventy thousand words in three weeks, probably in a near trancelike state (488).

Another similarity between the poem "Sullen Moods" and Graves's later writings, especially those concerned with the Goddess, is the utter dependence of Graves as poet (and as man) on the love and will of the Woman/Muse/Goddess. His acceptance of her domination is unreserved, as he made clear in both "Sullen Moods" and in "Postscript 1960": "Being in love does not, and should not, blind the poet to the cruel side of woman's nature—and many Muse poems are written in helpless attestation of this by men whose love is no longer returned" (491). In "Sullen Moods" Graves had accepted that his love was "no longer returned" and questioned whether friendship could suffice. He seems to conclude that his dependence excludes the possibility of friendship.

"Sullen Moods" indicates the separation of Graves's everyday world from his emotional or spiritual one. A poem that originates from his desire to apologize to his wife for being in a bad mood becomes a contemplation of the ultimate meaning of life and art. The everyday world of making up with a tender quatrain and a box of chocolates or a bunch of flowers (dinner out if the mood was a really ripe one) falls to his spiritual despair, as in "A Valentine," that devastating poem of dependent love. In fact or in fancy, Graves had stepped into the supranormal.

In revising this poem, Graves expressed and rejected what seemed to trouble him most: what he felt for wife and children and, predictably, what he felt for himself. By the late drafts, Graves has decided to remove all but the apology, one which leaves out the real concern of the poem, the door which trauma opened for him: a desire to be directed by a woman strong enough to rule without recourse to love or friendship or marital obligation. In revising, Graves followed the act of the poet as he described it in "Definitions," the first chapter of *On English Poetry* (1922), his first published critical study of poetry. To move through revision from a poem coming from "the unforeseen fusion in his [the poet's] mind of apparently contradictory emotional mesmerism" to "the more-or-less deliberate attempt, with the help of a rhythmic mesmerism to impose an illusion of actual experience on the minds of others" (13). The appearance of the nucleus, then, may well be transformed as the poet revises. In the case of "Sullen Moods," Graves acknowledged his deep despair and his hope of healing.

Throughout *Whipperginny*, Graves presents love as traumatic and dangerous but a balm, the giving of which rests with the woman. Though he does not say so openly, he desires a strong, dominant woman who will give what she promises, as in "Song of Contrariety":

> In the presence empty air,
> In the spectre clay,
> That Love, lent substance by despair,
> Wanes, and leaves you lonely there
> On the bridal day? (5)

In this poem, Graves finds love only in his dreams and hauntings. For Graves, poet, has found his subject in the hauntings that came from war and sex. What marriage promised (at least in his mind) has been performed for the man, and the poet has been healed by the willingness of the woman to accept responsibility for his health, indeed for his life. Quite likely, neither Nancy Nicholson nor any one woman could have met Graves's expectations, especially as the poem itself explains the process by which the healing has occurred: her consent as flesh and blood during the waking hours of day fades to be replaced in empty air by "spectre clay," a spirit as tangible as clay and clay as intangible as spirit. She is not tangible to sight and touch as to awareness in dream, and so his bridal union is a lonely one. He has not yet found the muse who could be the emissary of his goddess. No one woman will ever fill the part.

In ways the Georgians never knew, Graves vivified the poetry he inherited, a poetry of outworn images based on a reality he had seen literally blown to pieces. As he later observed, the poetry of Rupert Brooke died in the trenches of France. Men and women in Graves's poems are creatures of passion needing direction other than what his inherited reality can provide. In "The Ridge-Top" Graves moves his readers through the stages of past securities in a rural landscape to his present ambiguity. He describes a woman facing into the North Wind, whose "lusty force" molds her dress to her body and streams off her "set face."

> So now no longer flesh and blood,
> But poised in marble thought you stood,
> O Wingless Victory, loved of men,
> Who could withstand your triumph then? (6)

The lines of the poem, though bleak, should offer no surprises to an audience accustomed to the English poetry of the Georgians: landscape descriptions allow the poet to avoid less seemly images. Yet Edward Marsh found Graves's poetry from this era to be incomprehensible. The power of poetic unreason rather than rational development troubled him. But the dress molded to the woman's body by the wind introduces an unaccustomed physicality, which would also have troubled Marsh.

As he has done, Graves does again, refusing to let the woman be flesh and blood only. She becomes at best an ascendant goddess, at worst marble if one reads the poem as Graves's reducing his wife to armless inhumanity and inconsequence. A better reading, though, is that Graves is once again unable to find an adequate image for his spiritual reality. Though real, his experience is not of an individual. Though spiritual, it is not amorphous or abstract. Graves's feminine power does not yet have form and character in his writing, perhaps because he has not cleared his perception of the effects of traumas he could only express forcefully through analogy.

Without doubt, he expected his wife to heal his wounds and, ultimately, to move with him beyond the confines of flesh—an impossible expectation. In the early twenties, his marriage to Nancy was very stressful, but no biographer has suggested infidelity. And Graves denied such occurred before the arrival of Laura Riding. The life that occurs in the poems portrays a troubled, probably indecisive man who though chaste is looking for satisfaction greater than what could be given by any human companion. Freud's assertion that every dream is a wish is applicable to these poems that resonate with doubt and despair. Graves is aware of his need for a power greater than himself, one not susceptible to human frailty. His poems resonate with doubt that he can live in that spiritual presence, though he would accept her whims and wiles.

The single poem in *Whipperginny* that reveals Graves's concerns about chastity and fidelity is "Richard Roe and John Doe," an often republished poem about adultery and envy; or, we might say, the breaking of Commandments 7 and 10. Although Richard Roe envied Job, Solomon, and Alexander, he most envied the man who made him a cuckold, one John Doe. Graves would have the same experience within five years, so the poem may prefigure his life.

The word "prefigure" has appeared often enough in studies of Graves to deserve comment. The poet Graves could be seen as trading in mere coincidences or to be prescient. The term he preferred and used in *The White Goddess* was "analepsis," the ability of someone—poet, doctor, scientist—to make "a prodigious mental leap into the dark" and land "firmly on both feet" (334). Graves continues to explain that he knew the central truth of his book before he had established the proof, and he cites comparable discoveries of scientists.

"Richard Roe and John Doe" and many other poems indicate that Graves does not regard the roles of husband and wife as fixed and simple. Instead, they proceed from an understanding of self as potential, not a simple fixed role. As with the male and female personae he develops in his poem, so with the relationships between them: nothing is stable. Such, as well, is the view of such a high Modernist as James Joyce, whose Ulysses found himself at the beck and call of his wife, Molly Bloom. Joyce also recognized that a breaking down of Victorian public reality could destroy traditional gender roles. That Joyce came to such a view without a trauma similar to Graves's indicates, I think, the fact and force of that trauma within Western culture. Graves, as well as Joyce, was more than ready to accept a new faith, especially if he could himself carve the tablets and write the gospels. But psychological understanding was in its first flowering as thousands of psychologically wounded soldiers wandered the streets— often without treatment—and less often under the treatment of scientists such as W. H. R. Rivers. Joyce and Graves were fed by the same patriarchy and broke free in much the same way.

If "Richard Roe and John Doe" were Graves's only poem expressing his uncertainty, we might regard it as a flash of doubt, as we might regard Gabriel Conroy's similar doubt in Joyce's *The Dead*. It is, however, only one example of Graves's working out by character and plot his pleasurable anxiety about love in the way Rivers had said dreams work out the problems of the day. Though Graves's poems may have their resonance in his marriage, without doubt they reflect his belief, or need, that woman be dominant in matters of love and, as he will later write in *The White Goddess,* that the male determines neither the terms nor duration of the affair. Though he would not claim superiority to women, as in "Mirror, Mirror," he has not found the embodiment of the woman he senses, anticipates:

> Shall I marry a gentleman?
> Shall I marry a clown?
> Or shall I marry Old Knives-and-Scissors
> Shouting through the town? (36)

Woman here cannot choose, caught as she is in the patriarchy, a theme Graves repeats in "A History of Peace," which tells of the death in war of Henry Reece, but concludes with a condemnation of the world that brought about the soldier's death and the abuse of his mother. In this poem, Graves combines his war experience and Nancy's complaint about the traditional abuse of women. Underlying this and other poems is a concern that woman's real power, personal and sexual, cannot occur within a patriarchal society. Such a society regards women and children as property, the bond between men and women the legal contract of marriage.

So uncomfortable is the poet with such concerns that he only deals with them in personae who are often quite fantastic and seldom equated with himself. "An Idyll of Old Age" tells the story of the aged couple Baucis and Philemon, who dumbfound Zeus with their consideration of adultery. A surprisingly circumspect Zeus is shocked, but assuaged by Hermes, who assures Zeus the aged and infirm couple neither could nor would break their vows. If the poem were to end with a reassuring comment, it might well be read simply as Graves's practicing his poetic art by retelling an old tale. But as narrator, he provides a reason for the tale other than the practice of poetry. Lacking a sense of humor, the gods fail to understand that Baucis and Philemon, though sexually inert, repeat "conflicts of an earlier heat" (43).

Almost all other poems about love and sex in this volume are written about such "conflicts." Graves appears to sense the approach of "time's winged chariot," and he knew well how quickly life can end. The fragility of life and love are constants in Graves's earlier poetry and continue as major themes. Never does he attempt to explain the fragility but simply indicates it as characteristic of our species. Woman chooses and man accepts, to paraphrase the title of his 1964 volume of poetry, *Man Does, Woman Is*.

Sound figures largely in Graves's poetry, as we saw in his discussion of "The Gnat" in *The Meaning of Dreams*. To reiterate: the sound of a gnat that had burrowed into a man's brain drove him crazy. "The 'Gnat' is an assertion that to be rid of the gnat (shell-shock) means killing the sheep dog (poetry)" (164). In *The Treasure Box* (1919), Graves uses sound similarly in "Catherine Drury." In "The Kiss," however, Graves exactly anticipates by ten years his use of sound in *The Shout* (1929). The short story tells a madman's tale of sound, fury, and love of three people who seek love and find a power so great their sense of self and their sanity is shaken, changed utterly. The narrative lacks a useful frame since Graves puts it in a madman's mouth, but "The Kiss," which tells the same tale, does provide an entree to that troubled tale:

> Is that Love? No, but Death,
> A passion, a shout,
> The deep in-breath,
> The breath roaring out,
> And once that is flown,
> You must lie alone,
> Without hope, without life,
> Poor flesh, sad bone. (TB 8)

Graves only reprinted this powerful love poem once, two years later in *The Pier-Glass*. Since he generally revised poems he reprinted often, perhaps he chose not to go back to a poem with such problems: the poetic abstractions of "Death" and "Love," the repetition of the femme fatale, the self-conscious philosophizing on first causes which anticipates the philosophic inquiries he would soon begin with Basanta Mallik (to which he would likewise never return). "The Kiss," though, is central to understanding Graves's love poems and his understanding of love at this time.

Travelers are known by the baggage they carry; and Graves was carrying much from the nineteenth century, mainly the idea of love as humanity's most noble achievement and the ideal medium of all a poet has to write, whether it be a love for humanity and a love for another, as was the case in Elizabeth Barrett Browning's poems, or a love for the self written in the form of love for another as in Tennyson's *In Memoriam*. The example of these poets and the language of the Romantics, especially Keats, young Graves would have inherited through his father and his uncle. But he would not have inherited from them the dangerous passion described in "The Kiss." That would have come directly from such an experience as Keats had with Fanny Brawne, or at least as he presented that experience in "La Belle Dame Sans Merci." As Graves has so often written, such a complex and overwhelming passion exceeds the human, making the man and woman merely its medium.

Graves, the poet traveling in the realms of love, extended that moment of passion by rhythm and image into a poem. Yet when he came to write of the new world he had entered, he was inarticulate. In a significant short story, *The Shout* (1929), Graves wrote of a troubling affair between a woman and two men with the trauma of love and fear expressed in a life-destroying shout from one of the men. The image of a shout that he cannot describe and his readers cannot imagine was for Graves, at this time and for years to come, the only expression of the other possible. The mystic's life has not found form. To a great extent, it never will, and Graves's only option will be the historic re-creation of the matriarchy and its ultimate expression for him, the White Goddess.

Through his images of sound that can overwhelm reason and even the body itself, Graves creates metaphors that give readers a sense of the powers about which he is writing. I believe he chose sound, very loud sound, because such sound figured so largely in the changed circumstance of his life. He went from a quiet, bucolic (very Georgian) environment to one of mechanized warfare with its noise of bombardment and men shouting. Eventually, sound became his image for the trauma of shell shock, and sound, in this case the shout, became his image for the trauma of love. Under the force of such traumas, Graves's reason no longer could direct his writing; and he became a proponent of the concept reflected in the title of his revised undergraduate thesis, *Poetic Unreason.*

Even though *Whipperginny* was not published until 1923, many of the poems can actually be dated as written in 1921 (including "Sullen Moods," discussed above). The poems in this volume have more in common with each other than they do with the poems in the next two volumes: *The Feather Bed* and *Mock Beggar Hall.* Hauntings as occur in these later volumes are intended as re-creations of historical events. For example, "Witches" purports to retell the story of Agnes Sampson, who confessed to the king about flying with witches on "the night of All Hallow E'en" in 1591. Later Graves will write historical fiction to re-create past times and people, and will disguise his concerns more so than he does in "Witches." *I, Claudius* and *Claudius the God* are easily read as studies of the unrestrained exercise of power, especially by autocratic women. When he wrote the novels, he was living with Laura Riding, surely a reliable subject for any study of the exercise of power.

The powers of love in the three preceding volumes of poetry are here as well, but not in haunted intensity. Though no less concerned with love's dangers and the fragility of life, Graves was able in these volumes for Hogarth to remove, or repress, the persona of the sunken-eyed neurotic staring at his readers from mirrors. Yet his sense of sin and awareness of the church of his youth remain, as in "The North Window" from *Mock Beggar Hall*, set on the Eve of All Souls. Graves notes that "suicides too have souls" and then lists the damned who rise: "infants unbaptized" and their betrayed mothers who murdered them, all found in the scene on the North Window that portrays the "Creator who damns" and thrusts to the left the sheep and lambs, and on the right, "the goats and kids accursed" (13). The speaker is angry with the morality of the Christianity of his youth but is yet unable to free himself from it. The "greater detachment in the poet and the appearance of a new series of problems in religion, psychology and philosophy" (v), which Graves saw in the later poems of *Whipperginny*, are characteristic of *The Feather Bed* and *Mock Beggar Hall*. He had not yet said good-bye to the Christianity of his childhood. In 1921 Graves probably could not have presented those denied salvation without assuming their identity, without living in their personae. By this time, however, the neurotic intensity has been replaced with a self-aware playing of roles, with blatant discussions of contemporary (often faddish) philosophic concerns. His rambling explanation of *The Feather Bed* in "Introductory Letter To John Ransome [*sic*], The American Poet," more accurately refers to the change initiated, for a period of a few volumes, with Hogarth. Graves, who previously over-explained, simply wrote:

> Still the poem is a necessary signpost to those friends of mine who have found the change between the two halves of my recent collection of lyrics, *Whipperginny*, inexplicably abrupt: and though dissatisfied I am not ashamed. (5)

The change occurred because Graves and family moved from Boar's Hill to Islip, where the Graveses seem to have been less troubled, less intensely rattled by each other. Problems with money continued, for Graves was determined to make his living as a writer, to be in the employ of no one. The family, especially his mother, often aided them financially. Though the family was still financially unstable, an air of bucolic bonhomie existed. There remained access to luxury, invitations to Lady Ottoline Morrell's home, Garsington, and to his family's homes in London and Wales. Nancy refused to go to Garsington, and Graves's prediction that she would be a mother to Sassoon and other poet friends faded. Yet his loyalty was to Nancy, which he repeatedly made clear to Sassoon, as in this letter from Islip in February of 1921: "Nancy is much easier to get on with now, everybody seems to agree, especially if no particular effort is made to smooth her down" (BCNYPL). The household could not have been an easy one for either Nancy or Robert.

Curiously, Graves retained few of the poems from this (relatively) stable time in his life. Most did not survive past *Poems (1914–1926)*. The longest, and presumably the most demanding, were not reprinted: "Mock Beggar Hall" and "Interchange of Selves" by Basanta Mallik, with editing and "Prologue" by Graves. Concerns seen in *Whipperginny* with international and national politics, with economics and theories of civilization, dominate these poems, suggesting an alliance with pacifists Graves would not repeat. He reprinted two as late as *Robert Graves Poems* in 1980: "Full Moon" and "Myrrhina." "Myrrhina" tells a rather obtuse tale of a woman who comes to understand that the pain of a whale to produce ambergris for her perfume and of an oyster to produce pearls for her decoration replicates, as well, the price she will pay for beauty: Yeats's observation that "We must labor to be beautiful" comes to mind here (89). The effort to achieve and maintain the appearance of beauty cuts into the very self: society will be paid. Though not mentioned in the poem, the conflict between the beauties of self and those of tradition will occupy Graves throughout his life. But by far, the most important of the poems Graves continued to reprint is "Full Moon," which tells of the poet's awareness of the dominance of the goddess, the moon, as he walks "out one harvest night." There, "a tedious owlet" and "a nightingale" are to him:

> Like man and wife who nightly keep
> Inconsequent debate in sleep
> As they dream side by side.

Such a passage recalls the transformation of flesh and blood to spirit during dream in "Song of Contrariety." And in "Interchange of Selves," even under the influence of Basanta Mallik and his theories of peace, Graves held to the importance of dreams. In fact, he increased their significance, as is expressed by the self called "Mysticus" who directs his companions to look into their dreams if they mean to build a "respectable" and "peaceful" society. In those dreams they will find "the roots of all the disintegrating forces" and "all the storm centers that ever arose in the past" (47). Those impediments to peace are like Stephen Dedalus's view of history: a "nightmare" from which one tries to awaken (35). "Mock Beggar Hall," an emblem of British culture cast as nightmare or dream, indicates the importance Graves attached to dream. It tells the tale not only of the individual's self or the "inconsequent debate" (probably inconsequent only because it concerns spirit not clay) between husband and wife, but also of the culture's self. Dream goes perhaps to the core of life itself.

The last three stanzas of "Full Moon" certainly intend to go well beyond the everyday life of the poet and his wife. Though this poem has traces of Graves's political concerns and is resonant of the ghostly love poems of incubi and succubi, Graves leads away from the personal to an awareness of the source of love itself: phantoms (what he had called both ghosts and phantasms). They come as spectres to give life to clay from a spirit greater even than themselves:

> To cloud the eager flame of love,
> To fog the shining gate:
> They held the tyrannous queen above
> Sole mover of their fate;
> They glared as marble statues glare
> Across the tesselated stair. . . . (8)

This tale might well have been told by Coleridge's ancient mariner, for it has the eerie sense of the fragility of human desire in the grand scheme of things. Quite likely written about his marriage, the players have spiritual as well as physical roles, "spectre" as well as "clay." Both the woman and the poet have a "phantom" and wear "the moon's cold mask," the manifestation of the Goddess. In this poem, more than in any he would ever write, Graves gave voice to the terror and awe that the woman, the muse, felt. As with the poet, the muse is possessed and at risk. Here more complexly than ever before, Graves articulated his awareness of the Goddess. In "Full Moon," Graves describes the Goddess's subjects and the land she rules and pledges himself to her tyranny.

Graves had written of the Goddess before, but had always drawn back into personal narrative. Here the final metaphors lead away from, not to, his own everyday life. Whatever happened during the time he wrote *Mock Beggar Hall* enabled him to look with awe, but not fear, into the workings of things, such as politics and culture. But of even greater importance, he looked, again with awe though not fear, into the spiritual. "Practicus," another of the selves in "Interchange of Selves," in trying to explain "the most gruesome and insistent fact, that caprice turns the wheel of life as much as reason does" (55), reveals a new openness for Graves's persona. "Caprice," or what Graves also had called the "Non-Aristotelian" nature of reality (perceived by the freely associative mind), does not receive the insistent attention of "evil." After all, "caprice" may let "evil" gain power, but "reason" could as well, as Graves's condemnation of the cause and practices of World War I indicated.

The important issues in this section from "Interchange of Selves" are that Graves has admitted the existence of forces greater than his own unconscious, greater than perceived history. Though speaking through a persona, he has admitted his concern with "Witchcraft." This play(let) Graves developed from a manuscript of Basanta Mallik that lacked punctuation, paragraphs, and scenes. Mallik did not care in what form the piece evolved since the purpose of his writing was "of informing him [Graves] of the nature of a series of metaphysical cruces." So informed, Graves wanted to hold to the idea of distinct personae, though Basanta Mallik said:

> In the end, when each has momentarily domi-
> nated and been defeated by the others, there will
> be no practical man, no mystic and no com-
> promiser left on the stage. Neither virtue nor
> villainy will prevail. (MBH 38)

Neither then nor later was Graves willing to be so unjudgmental. In "Historical Commentary" at the end of *King Jesus* (1946), Graves used the word "iconotropy" to define a practice in which "the icons are not defaced or altered, but merely interpreted in a sense hostile to the original cult" (423). Two years later in *The White Goddess,* Graves was more forceful in describing "iconotropy" with reference to the story of the judgment of Paris. Tradition has it that the young shepherd awarded the apple to Aphrodite, preferring her to either Hera or Athene. Graves viewed this reading of the icon of the four figures as a willful misinterpretation. In his view, the three goddesses were actually "the three persons of the ancient Triple Goddess, not jealous rivals, and obviously the Love-goddess is giving the apple to the Shepherd (or goat-herd), not receiving it from him" (249–250). In this example, iconotropy comes about as the patriarchy displaces the matriarchy. Graves believed that "villainy" was real and present; he accepted having to struggle against it. He was, however, always capable of playing any of the three roles: mystic, compromiser, practical man. Part of his effort as man and writer was to make all serve the same mistress.

Graves's biographers unanimously name Laura Riding as that mistress, though Graves loved and served others before and after her, and none so long as his second wife, Beryl. Yet there is another problem in assigning to one woman the title of mistress, as Graves indicated in his dedication to *Poems (1914–1926)*: "For N. and L." Perhaps convention dictated he would dedicate the volume to his wife as well as the recently met Laura Riding, or perhaps he was unsatisfied with only one woman in his life. "Pygmalion to Galatea" supports such a view of Graves. Included in the last section of *Poems (1914–1926)*, it was first published in *The London Mercury* (10–11 May 1926). The artist, Pygmalion (persona of the poet Graves, we assume), as he turned his ideal into flesh, was excited, a bit apprehensive, and quite certain of his expectations, physical and moral:

> "As you are woman, so be lovely:
> Fine hair afloat and eyes irradiate,
> Long lovely fingers, fearless carriage,
> And body lissom, neither small nor tall;
> So be lovely! (201–203)

As photographs of Nancy and Laura show, if Graves were speaking through Pygmalion, he did not get the woman described; but in conventional terms, love is blind. And Graves was exceedingly conventional in his view of woman until he cast her in the role of murderess and dominatrix. Later when he wrote of her in *The White Goddess,* he would be even more unconventional in his portrait of a woman as ideal. He would abandon, too, Pygmalion's expectations of her character, that she be discreet, for instance, merciful and constant (202). Graves met Laura Riding 2 January 1926, and less than five months later was hinting at "stairway gossip." Having resigned his university post, Graves, two women, and four children returned after six months in Cairo. The gossip was out of the stairwell, out of the window in fact. In the revised edition of *Good-Bye To All That,* Graves omitted these melodramatic paragraphs in the 1928 version:

> After which.
> After which, anecdotes of yours, travesties of the parable and so precious to me as vulgar glosses on it. How on April 27th,
>   1929 it was a fourth-storey window and a stone area and

you were dying. And how it was a joke between Harold
the stretcher-bearer and myself that you did not die, but
survived your dying, lucid interval.
After which.
After which, may I recall, since you would not care to do so yourself,
with what professional appreciation (on May 16th) Mr.
Lake is reported to have observed to those that stood by
him in the operating theatre: 'It is rarely that one sees the
spinal-cord exposed to view—especially at right-angles to
itself.' (322–323)

If Graves did not get the discretion in love he hoped for in 1926, neither
did he get the variety and constancy Galatea promised Pygmalion.

Young Graves was unable to comprehend the world, having been over-
protected by his mother and by his class. Until he entered the army, Graves
had little open acquaintance with men who did not respect (or at least
protect) his idyll. In the army, he was odd, an outsider, as Sassoon observed. Unfashionable, aloof, unliked—all these protected his innocence.
Closely tied to a view of self and England, his innocence was based on the
public virtues of Victorian England: duty, chastity, honor. A woman, such
as Virginia Stevens Woolf, learned early on that these public virtues did
not direct behavior inside the house, where she was verbally abused by her
father and at age ten was sexually abused by her step-brother. Graves was
spared such an early, violent end to his childhood, but as he saw Victorian
England played out in the trenches, he did desire a different and more
honest world. As he would do throughout his life, Graves the poet would
remake the world of Graves the man.

The poet would be busy, for Graves's loves and loyalties would change
drastically, often obliterating the work the poet had done in creating an
agreeable context and persona for self and others. I recall saying to Graves
that I thought one of the poems in *Love Respelt* was written to the
Goddess:

"Well, that's quite possible. Which one?"
"Dancing Flame."
"Oh, no. That was written to a Mexican woman who behaved very
badly, very badly indeed."

Graves did not anticipate a muse as unpredictable as Marie Laraçuen, the
Mexican woman referred to above. The years with Laura Riding had been

tempestuous, demanding, but she stayed rather much in her role: a woman morally opposed to "population activities" (i.e., sex) until she met Schyler Jackson in 1939. In scenes that nearly destroyed Jackson's wife, Kit, Laura cut all her ties with Graves and took Schyler Jackson, with whom she would spend the rest of her life (Matthews 201–220).

By 1941, Beryl and Robert were living in England, and the second Graves family was soon to begin. There would be four children: William, Lucia, Juan, and Tomas. Beryl would provide Graves with a stable, and protected, life in which muses would be present but not disruptive. But then there was that Mexican woman who behaved badly.

Whether Graves in his early love poems predicted, anticipated, or caused the difficulties he had with women, we cannot know. Quite clearly, though, when he opened the door into the unconscious, he found demons he does not seem to have met in his waking life. So powerful were these that they would prefigure the most powerful experience of his life and writing: the White Goddess, the ultimate reality of his "mind-life" and his poetry. The muse never became the Goddess but remained a representative, mere flesh and bones; yet she would reflect the whimsical and unpredictable Goddess, giving and withholding affection without explanation. Graves was more likely to celebrate such treatment in his poetry than to accept it in his life—as his comment about that "Mexican woman" indicates. And that we all share with Robert Graves. What we do not share, most of us anyway, with Graves is his actual meeting with "the death-white Fay." And so we must decide whether to accept the word of a man seemingly obsessed with speaking the truth about his life, or to reject it because we cannot apply the scientific test of authenticity to it. It cannot be replicated at will, though circumstances may be at play here. Whether we accept Graves's statements as true or not, we must acknowledge the experiences, the traumas, that prepared him for such experiences.

CHAPTER 6

THE POET

Classical is characteristic and Romantic is Metaphoric, that is though they are both expressions of a mental conflict, in Classical poetry this conflict is expressed within the confines of waking probability and logic, in terms of the typical interaction of typical minds; in Romantic poetry the conflict is expressed in the illogical but vivid method of the dream-changings.

On English Poetry

Robert Graves was always a Romantic poet, shaped first by the language of Keats's poems and then by the reality that haunted them. As is probably true for all of us, Graves first saw Keats through Victorian eyes. That good Victorian, his father, gave him the Everyman edition of Keats's poems that he carried with him to France, the volume in which he wrote his own very sensory poems about war and the memories it aroused. At first, he wrote of the trauma of war, the insane denial of reason, and found ghosts he would have preferred to believe were "condensations" of his troubles into dramatic figures. He worked very diligently in *Poetic Unreason* and *The Meaning of Dreams* to convince his readers (and himself) that his hauntings were the mechanics of the unconscious at work solving the problems of the day with the dreams of the night, holding to reasonable answers of unreasonable problems. When depth psychology did not relieve his trauma, and he admitted that he did not want relief, Graves rejected psychology. He did not, however, acknowledge elsewhere than in his poems that he accepted the creatures who haunted him as his spiritual reality. Though I have written "creatures," more properly I should write "the Goddess." Graves's acceptance of the reality of the Goddess was a more important shaping force on his poetic than any of the schools to which he claimed passing alliance: Victorian, Georgian, Modernist.

Handwritten labels on photograph: Sam Jenny Nancy Catty Robert David.

Robert Graves, Nancy Nicholson, Jennie Nicholson, Catherine Nicholson, David Graves, and Sam Graves at World's End Cottage in 1924

As was true for Samuel Butler, Graves's early idol, young Graves chose not to accept the press to enter one of the family's traditional professions: clergy or civil service. Instead he early on turned to the vocation of poetry, as Butler turned to art. Fortunately for Graves, his father was well-known for his own poetic achievements—especially for the popular song "Father O'Flynn." Thus, Graves did not encounter either Butler's abuse by his father or his banishment. But Butler and Graves shared the experience of families locked in Victorian thought and propriety, and both writers rebelled. Most likely young Graves agreed with Butler's doubting of the literal veracity of the biblical miracles and of Christianity itself, though in *My Head! My Head!* (Graves's first novel), he wrote of the miracles performed by Elijah, Elisha, and Moses as the work of great magicians. As much as Graves protested about the Victorian influence of father and uncle, this belief in the spiritual probably came through them to young Graves. Understandably, a young man of talent would want to go his own way, as he indicated in a letter to Edward Marsh on 19 March 1915. He hoped that Marsh and the Georgians would help him become modern, free him from the Victorian influence of his family. Wanting very much to be part of the new Georgian poetry, Graves frequently wrote March letters extolling the poetry and life of Rupert Brooke, comparing Brooke's fascination with the South Sea Islanders with that of:

> My great spiritual father Samuel Butler put them among the three comeliest (unreadable)and best bred peoples of the world; I am astonished how Butler overshadows & colours all life for me; never a day passes but I think of him in a score of connections just as Handel overshadowed & coloured life for Butler himself—That's why I was so pleased with Rupert for quoting the Discobolus in connection with Montreal because for me that poem is the only thing that makes the town live. (BCNYPL)

Not yet twenty, Graves can be forgiven for being overawed in the aura of Georgians; yet even so young, he never praised Brooke's talent, although his subject matter and his sensitivity, yes. And if in tone Graves seems to cavil, that too can be forgiven. Graves clearly wished to have Marsh approve of him as he had of Brooke. In asking Marsh to be his literary executor and to have complete authority to change his poems, Graves mimicked Brooke, who named Marsh his literary executor, an ineffectual one because of the control exercised by Brooke's mother. In Graves's rapid growth as poet, the force of his father dwindled, and he accepted Marsh, whom he called the "Father of Modern Poetry," as his own poetic father, granting him greater authority than had Brooke. Graves would never completely lose the imprint of these two men: Butler because of such iconoclastic works as *Erewhon,* with its mixture of satire and utopianism that Graves would reflect in *Watch the North Wind Rise* (1949); Marsh because Graves would ever be a poet of the English countryside and the privileged classes. In spite of his complaining after the fact, Graves was deeply indebted to his father, who worked without recognition to get his young son accepted. He not only pursued Edward Marsh concerning his son's future, but arranged for Harold Monro of the Poetry Bookshop to publish *Over the Brazier.* Since Monro was publisher of the Georgian poetry anthologies, Graves's first book was set well.

Sir James George Frazer, or more particularly Frazer of *The Golden*

Bough, was equally important in imprinting the young Graves, who would also follow the gentlemanly vocation of what now might be called a cultural anthropologist. Like Frazer, Graves would look closely into history, religion, and myth without fear of losing his own capacity to believe in the miraculous. The methods of the Victorian scientist were not lost on young Graves, who believed that poetry was to be discussed scientifically, yet without losing one's sense of awe. Years later, he would as well instruct the faculty and students of the Massachusetts Institute of Technology on their obligations. Understandably, they found him a prickly guest, as did Bruno Freidman, who interviewed him for the journal *Impact of Science on Society*:

Interviewer: Mr. Graves, as a poet, classical scholar, and novelist whose books are based on the ancient Greek and Roman civilization, you are particularly qualified to look at modern science from a historical perspective.

I'd like to start by referring to an intriguing remark you made in a letter addressed to *Impact* a few weeks ago. You wrote: "Science ceased to be what it pretended to be, an idealistic search for wisdom, some time in the thirteenth century—though some insist on back-dating this to the twelfth." What did you mean by that?

Graves: Just what I said. Science has lost its virgin purity, has become dogmatic, instead of seeking for enlightenment and has gradually fallen into the hands of traders. I was thinking of alchemy, which in its original form was a humble search for knowledge and truth based on intuition, but was gradually taken over by perverters and frauds who sought to persuade kings that they could turn base metal into gold. (*Conversations* 81)

Graves as he matured, aged, continued to tip the lance at what he considered cultural error, and the young man who published *Over the Brazier* in 1916 had not completely abandoned the spirit and ideas of his late-Victorian foster fathers. Decorative classical motifs would appear in his poetry for years, but by the time of the above interview, Graves was committed to reliving the past, not with using it for rhetorical flourishes.

Young Graves would comfortably publish "The Dying Knight and the Fauns," juvenilia from Charterhouse, which lacks even the conservative enlightenment of the Georgians:

Woodland fauns with hairy haunches
Grin in wonder through the branches
Woodland fauns that know no fear (OB 7)

Graves here sees Keats through the grieving Tennyson's ambiguous attraction to pleasure slightly tweaked by a schoolboy's infatuation with fin de siècle malaise. Odd, though, is his mention of the hallucinogenic mushroom so early in his life. In the 1960s and 1970s, his interest would become personal as well as literary. He would incorporate the taking of this drug into his discussion of Greek religion, in particular the two births of Dionysus and the worship of Dionysus (DQEA 104–112). Perhaps his interests in the Romantics had taken him beyond their poetry and into their practices. Coleridge, to mention only one, certainly took opium.

Though he had in *On English Poetry* discussed his fondness for Keats by applying the precepts of psychology to literary criticism, of more moment is his explanation in *Poetic Unreason* of his preferring Keats to Shelley. Keats's "tactile qualities" and "his appeal to the senses of taste and smell" most attracted Graves, whereas he saw in Shelley "an appeal to the sense of motion" to which he was "unsympathetic" for reasons based on his own "personal history" (267). The train trip Graves endured after his wounding at the Somme seriously affected his capacity to travel for some years and, as illustrated by his view of Shelley's poetry, influenced his critical judgment as well. Such a change could be, should be, considered an accidental rather than an essential characteristic of Graves. But he would forever hold to this assertion from the last chapter of *Poetic Unreason*: "And when I come to consider it, all the poems which mean so much more to me than to others, have, without exception, this tactile quality" (270). By such attention to tactile qualities rather than the focus of the poem or the views of the poet, Graves acknowledged that readings might well diverge from the author's intent—a possibility he accepted. The uncomprehended meanings hidden by conflict and condensation might well escape the poet's intentionality, though Graves would never assert, as did Eliot and Pound, that the poem and not the poet was all important. Always for Graves, the poet, even if in a state of trance, made possible the poem.

The poems from Graves's first volumes were highly tactile, concerned as they were with his experience with the war. Uncertain whether he wrote for fellow soldiers or for the people back home (his wider audience), Graves wrote poems intended to give the flavor of the soldier's life but not alienate his civilian readers. In these poems, he struggled, generally unsuccessfully, to free himself from the attitudes about life, love, and art that had formed him. "To Robert Nichols," which he wrote a few months before being wounded at the Somme, has all the Keatsian tactile quality and all the feel of the little England so dear to the Victorians and to the Georgians. Even writing about the trenches in France, Graves holds to a poetic diction firmly set in the rhetoric of the Victorians and writes of "a snowbound river" beside which he and the other soldiers shiver in "scrapen holes." The conclusion of this section indicated that Graves held to such diction, perhaps to ward off the terrible experience of the war by recalling a past he probably feared was lost:

> Sleek fauns and cherry time,
> Vague music and green trees,
> Hot sun and gentle breeze,
> England in June attire,
> And life born young again. (20)

Still very imitative and learning his craft, Graves did not hesitate to paraphrase Keats without improving him as he describes a fruitful land losing all vital signs, as did Keats in "La Belle Dame Sans Merci," which ends memorably with "And no bird sings." That Graves's poem, as well, echoed Keats's "To Autumn" is clear:

> And touch the stubble plains with rosy hue;
> Then in a wailful choir the small gnats mourn
> Among the river sallows, home aloft
> Or sinking as the light wind lives or dies;
> And full-grown lambs loud bleat from hilly bourn.
> Hedge crickets sing, and now with treble soft
> The redbreast whistles from a garden croft
> And gathering swallows twitter in the skies. (360)

The longing so associated with Keats serves Graves well in his poem to Robert Nichols, a poem in which he has reason to consider the brevity of life: his own, his friend's, and John Keats's.

Graves's grounding in England (not Great Britain) and his deep commitment to the tradition of English verse define his poetic technique and utterly separate him from the poets and thinkers gathered around Ezra Pound, a group early called the Imagists (and fellow travelers): Richard Aldington, F. S. Flint, T. E. Hulme, T. S. Eliot. They and Graves shared a commitment to tactile images; and both inclined toward "the language that men speak," as had Wordsworth and Coleridge almost a hundred years earlier. But Graves preferred the language spoken by his Romantic ancestors to that of the professional intellectuals who were his contemporaries. And there is often scant intellectual difference between the Romantics, Graves, and the Imagists, for they would all question, and reject, the reasonable reality of Aristotle. Though we now see the Georgians and the Imagists as different poetic species, they had the same ur-sources in their desire to revitalize modern poetry. But the Georgians wanted to keep both baby and bath water, while Pound et al. happily tossed them out the window.

The image of a dead land would occur frequently in Graves's early poems, as indeed it did in T. S. Eliot's and Ezra Pound's; yet Graves would lace his poems with terms evocative of war. The poetry Graves the soldier at war wrote is frequently touched by what might be thought of as the typical experience of typical men, if those men were such as fought in France. Indeed, Graves does write for their shared "typical" experience, which the people at home can only comprehend analogously by recalling their own nightmares; so the language of his poetry, as well as the reality, can still properly be called Romantic. In "It's A Queer Time" from *Over the Brazier* Graves abruptly and shockingly extracts the unknown from that conventional figure, the English milkmaid Elsie, ten years dead, who "comes tripping gaily down the trench" in the middle of an earth-shaking bombardment (29).

The experience of war strongly affected Graves's language by making it more contemporary (a temporary quality) and by making the tactile image come from his life, not from his reading. Very quickly, even his reading would become part of his experience; and even tales by Ovid would be colored by Graves's war neurosis. Then, too, the reality he presents cannot be explained, only presented. One dead maid a'skipping down a trench in France during an earth-shaking bombardment cannot be explained logically, not even by the psychology Graves would soon encounter in talks with W. H. R. Rivers. To say Elsie is the ghost of a lost past would probably not have meant much to young Graves, who was dazed both by the bombardment and the ghost. She would have been as easy to accept as the violence that controlled his life.

In *Fairies and Fusiliers,* Graves reprinted some poems from *Over the Brazier* and *Goliath and David,* poems that did little to advance his poetic. He continued the three strands he was trying to weave into a coherent whole: the language of the Romantics he had inherited, the experience of trench warfare, and the analogous method he would adapt to his use for years. Of the three, the analogy was most important, allowing him to move from the discursive to the illogical, to reject Aristotle and his teaching. Graves's most obvious early examples of the use of analogy are in "Nursery Memories" from *Over the Brazier,* those early poetic recollections of childhood's traumas and nightmares. As telling as those, however, is "On Finding Myself A Soldier":

> My bud was backward to unclose,
> A pretty baby-queen,
> Furled petal-tips of creamy rose
> Caught in a clasp of green. (18)

Expecting the rose when in bloom to be "coloured in as out / Like the flush of dawn on snow," he is shocked when it becomes one red with the heart "more red than blood." As well as the Keatsian tactile still-life, the image of this poem is of a Georgian English garden rose pulled untimely into the war. Resonant of Brooke's "The Soldier" and anticipating Owen's "Anthem for Doomed Youth," "On Finding Myself a Soldier" differs from even the very good poems of World War I by method. Never is war mentioned. As in Graves's most moving poems about the war, the effect of war rather than its appearance is the subject of the poem. The rose here has associations with Christ as well as with the English garden, signs of lost innocence that can only be expressed by analogy or symbol, as Yeats did in his poems in *The Rose.* A reasoned, linear narrative would not suit Graves's attraction for the tactile or his dislike of motion in poetry.

I find few indications in Graves's earliest writing that he thought beyond his rather simplistic ideas of the poet, but he may have. Perhaps thinking his audience would respond as he did to beauty turned horrible, Graves chose the image of the rose separated from narrative and character. He may well have thought that no reader could remain unmoved. He could not, however, have considered that his own understanding of Keats's poetry was still consciously limited to an appreciation of Keats's language. Perhaps in the unconscious, he knew that Keats's beauty masked terror, but he was years away from such an understanding of himself and his poetry. "On Finding Myself a Soldier" presents the horror of his experience, as did "Nursery Memories," not by describing actions but by indicating the nature of the effect of the actions. Reality is inner, memory. And through memory, Graves reveals a personal history much like Yeats's Ireland: able to be the medium for whatever is important in human experience. Graves, though, thought in terms of a personal and familial identity, not a national one; yet he did give readers the experience of his England.

One of those few indications that Graves was looking beyond the conventions of the Georgians he revealed in a letter of 27 May 1916 to Sassoon:

> I have just discovered a great poet, a chap called Skelton (1460–1525) of whom there's been no edition since 1843: a true Englishman and a man after my own heart; wrote beautiful doggerel nonsense, thoroughly irresponsible & delightful jingles, though the "First scholar in the land" according to Erasmus. (BCNYPL)

In 1927, Graves would edit *John Skelton (Laureate) 1460?–1529*, one of the Augustan Books of English Poetry published by Benn. Skelton was a poet of the English countryside and English life. Graves included such light poems as "Jane Scroop's Lament for Phillip Sparrow," a pet killed by her cat Gib. But he also printed poems that showed Skelton's knowledge of Latin and Greek myth (reflecting Graves's own interests). And one poem strikes resonances in Graves's own obsessions, *"From 'On the Death of King Edward the Fourth,'"* in which Skelton presents Lady Fortune in terms familiar to Graves:

> She took me by the hand and led me a dance
> And with her sugared lippes on me she smiled;
> But, what for her dissembled countenance
> I could not beware till I was beguiled:
> Now from this world she hath me exiled
> When I was lothest hence for to go,
> And I am in age but (as who saith) a child,
> *Et ecce nunc in pulvere dormio.* . . . (13)

Skelton is an unusual taste for as young and derivative a poet as Graves was in 1916. But he would grow into Skelton, becoming himself a man familiar with the great—both in the material world and in that of the spirit.

Even in the poems Graves wrote when he was openly affiliating himself with the Georgians, Graves's poetry differed from that of the quintessential Georgian, Rupert Brooke, who held to the Victorian idea that literature should confine itself to a public reality. The decline in the reputation of Brooke and the Georgians may well have occurred because of this distancing of their inner life from their poetry. In "The Great Lover" Brooke wrote of *things* that defined this public reality, not his own inner torment. Graves in "1915" did write like a wet schoolboy. In his correspondence with Marsh, Graves would frequently ask his mentor to relay his greetings to "Dick," whom in correspondence he referred to by his own name, Peter. That Graves and all his friends knew each other is clear. Increasingly in his poetry, Graves would present love as passionate and illogical with no apologies to decorum or Aristotle. Here he and Edward Marsh would disagree.

What Graves shared, throughout his life, with the Georgians was an idea of England (Great Britain was a geographical and political concept with which he did not identify himself). He accepted the Royals, the conservatism of Churchill, the public school, the university commons, and even the regimental mess. For Graves, as he said about the Georgians, poetry "was to be English yet not aggressively imperialistic" (SMP 119). Early Graves, at least, was in agreement with Marsh's own description of the poetry he chose to champion and publish in the Georgian anthologies:

> I was, of course, guided by the preferences which instinct and training had formed in my mind; and these can be easily, if roughly, set forth. I liked poetry to be all of three (Or if not all three, at least two; or if the worst came to the worst at least one) of the following things: intelligible, musical and racy; and I was happier with it if it was written on some formal principle which I could discern, and from which it departed, if at all, only for the sake of some special effect, and not because the lazy or too impetuous writer had found observance difficult and irksome. I liked poetry that I wanted to know by heart, and *could* learn by heart if I had time. ("Prefatory Note," *Georgian Poetry* 322)

By "formal principle," Marsh probably meant a sonnet such as Brooke's "The Soldier." But "formal principle" implies even more: a reasonableness and discreteness of ideas. Paradox did not figure in Marsh's aesthetic, and paradox would become very important to Graves.

Young Graves was well connected with the most important poets of his day, as he indicated in this letter to Sassoon on 3 July 1917:

> I forgot the Poet Laureate likes Robert Graves' work too (not only S.S's) & sent a special congratulatory message to him through the mouth of Masefield. (BCNYPL)

Robert Bridges, the Poet Laureate, would probably have read the war poems Graves published in periodicals in 1916 and 1917 rather than his juvenilia, most of which Graves wisely did not reprint. Of the older contemporaries, Bridges, like Graves, preferred Keats. The poems of all have a fondness for tactile imagery which, perhaps, will always keep them current, for they tell of their time. Graves had received notice in journals as well as in the private comments of poets. As he wrote to Sassoon on 23 June 1916:

> The *Spectator* gives me over a column. Stating "Mr. R. G's verses have a quality which renders them memorable" & signed J. St. L. S. The *Times Litt. Supp.* Talk of a "complete sincerity which allows no hint of the imitative: if its rawness is sometimes repelling yet as the writer has an ear for musical cadence he often lays a spell on the reader & achieves something like true beauty . . . something new in the world of fancy. . . ." The *Nation* shuffles & refuses "to predict anything certain . . . from such immaturity. If he will develop a broader & deeper temper & perceive that flexibility is a means not an end he should do excellent work." (BCNYPL)

Graves is making his way, even into Harold Monro's Poetry Bookshop, home to Marsh and publisher of *Georgian Poetry*. Graves's father had arranged for Monroe to publish *Over the Brazier* in 1916. So the young Graves was on his way, especially if he did not deviate too far from the poems that won him such approval. Soon he would not only deviate, but go in a completely different direction, though continuing to be tactile in imagery and English in attitude. But he would not deviate from his dislike of Ezra Pound, which began long before he met the American in Lawrence's rooms at All Souls. Pound and Marsh thoroughly detested one another, as in fact Pound did all of those associated with Georgianism, with the slight exception of Monroe and, oddly, Rupert Brooke. Though Graves's poetic would take him far from Georgianism, he would never forget Edward Marsh. If Graves had one constant and immutable quality, it was the tenacity of his friendship, though he never allowed it to draw him into fruitless battles, as is witnessed by his not becoming a combatant in the struggle between Richard Aldington and Basil Liddell-Hart.

Liddell-Hart organized a campaign to stop publication of Aldington's biography of T. E. Lawrence, *Lawrence of Arabia: A Biographical Enquiry,* which discussed Lawrence's illegitimacy and his homosexuality. Though Liddell-Hart used all his contacts from Churchill to Graves, he was unable to stop publication. He did succeed in forcing Aldington to leave England because of a greatly reduced income. His books were removed from shops, and editors refused to see him. Of particular interest in this battle, though, is the element of class warfare, which Aldington's daughter Catherine told me was her father's view of the turmoil caused by his book. Aldington belonged to the new class of professional intellectuals, and Graves to the privileged classes for whom poetry was an essential part of a gentleman's accomplishment (or affectation), but not a commodity to be manufactured or traded. Though Graves the successful poet said he only made cigarette money from poetry, the young poet was more concerned with making his living as a writer—of poetry if possible. Graves's later high road was made possible by extremely popular prose. But the difference in attitudes of Graves and Aldington in 1955, when *Lawrence of Arabia: A Biographical Study* was published, does have its basis in a soul-deep difference, one that distinguished the two kinds of writers far more than their subjects: Graves would never don a banker's suit, as had T. S. Eliot, the ultimate professional intellectual of Graves's time.

The poems Graves wrote during the war do not substantively change from beginning to end, with the exception of "A Child's Nightmare," the poem about the blood-lapping cat that came to him while he was asleep. With this poem, Graves entered the unconscious without censoring it, though in his analysis of the poem in *Poetic Unreason*, he did attempt to lessen the terror by explanation. Though from the 1920s on he dismissed the authority of Aristotle, his explanation is rational since he still held to the scientist's finding of pattern as his way to truth. He had not yet accepted dream and vision as realities to be celebrated rather than explained. But the door into the unconscious had been opened, and with the guidance of Rivers, Graves would explore its primitive truth.

Graves was fortunate in his association with Rivers, though as Henry Head wrote to Graves on 7 April 1925, Rivers was unable to see the value of nonlogical thought, although late in life he saw "the creative value of intuitions, but as he had no intimate contact with poetry and was without sensory images, he naturally tended towards strictly logical forms of thinking" (UTHRC). Rivers admitted as much, but still Graves was better off than was the shell-shocked Septimus of Virginia Woolf's *Mrs. Dalloway*, whose doctors Woolf pilloried. They echoed the view of the Report of the War Office Committee of Enquiry in "Shell-shock" (1922), which recommended complete rest and a dedication of the patient to the manly virtues of control and proportion and the abandoning of self-interest for the greater good demanded by duty (Thomas 49–57). Graves survived, unlike Woolf's Septimus, who committed suicide, and the fatherly tolerance of Rivers may well have tipped the balance. Since Woolf met Graves in 1925, the year she published *Mrs. Dalloway*, she should have been more understanding and more receptive of him than she was. Septimus and Graves shared the same experiences and visions, and almost the same fate. Perhaps if Graves had not found sustaining visions in poetry, he too would have been a suicide. He, too, might have preferred oblivion to fright and despair.

Though the method of analogy could reconstruct the dream into a poem, the images themselves are as significant in revealing Graves's "mind-life" or spiritual reality. As the image was de rigeur for the Modernists, so it was for Graves, though increasingly his experience rather than his reading was the manifest, as well as the hidden, meaning of his poetry. Oddly, Graves and Pound both wrote intimately of the past, Graves in his historical novels and Pound in *The Cantos,* though Pound was more self-absorbed than Graves, who wrote more convincingly of the past. Unlike Eliot, who said the poem, not the poet, was important, Graves never denied that his poems reflected his life. Only recent criticism has told Eliot's own life story as it figures into his poetry, though as early as 1951 Rossell Hope Robbins made the connection in *The T. S. Eliot Myth.* Conventionally, as readers of poetry, we assume the poet extrapolates from life and finds expression in convenient genres. Whether Formalist or Freudian, such a reader assumes the poem does not tell the poet's actual and immediate experience. By the example of his own critical interpretations of poetry, and his own use of analogy, Graves facilitated such an approach to his own poetry. The poem may have its source in the poet's immediate experience of war, but its form and substance come from a distant memory, one to which he returned obsessively in dream. To paraphrase Wordsworth's dictum that poetry is "emotion recollected in tranquility," for Graves the poem is a nightmare recollected in terror. Yet Graves cannot present the power of the experience itself, instead needing a "formal principle," here the rhetorical one of analogy, to give expression to experience. Likewise in discussing "La Belle Dame Sans Merci" and his own poem "The Gnat," Graves oriented readers to consider the poems as analogies, not as direct expressions of the poet's experiences. As such, the poems do reflect, or refract, a life other than the poet's, a life that is expressed only in the poems. The major change in Graves's poetry will be his admission that not even poems can express that life since language by its very nature is conventional, not unique—no matter how great the writer.

In his discussions of these poems, Graves's own desire to make the poem convey experience through tactile language argues against the poem as analogy, as rhetorical convention.

For Graves, Keats's Merciless Lady is really Fanny Brawne, to whose teasing love Keats gave form and confinement through genre. In Graves's discussion these are no less important than his combining of history, psychology, and biography into literary criticism. Yet when Graves has said all, he remains troubled by the "kisses four" and cannot explain away their fact, their tactile existence:

> She took me to her elfin grot
> And there she wept and sighed full sore,
> And then I shut her wild wild eyes
> With kisses four. (271)

In *Poetic Unreason* (1925), Graves will repeatedly comment on Keats, whose poems have become part of "the familiar furniture" of his mind, mentioning again the appeal of Keats's poetry to "sense of touch" (272–274). Implied here is an attribution of the experience of the poem directly to the poet's experience, a rejection of convention, and an affirmation of a barely comprehensible reality. Such a reality can only be represented in tactile signs such as the specific number of kisses, which for the poet tell more than any words such as *love* or *rapture* or any description since the experience eludes capture.

In "Author's Note" to *Poetic Unreason,* Graves delineates his critical (and poetic) progression from "certain wayward notes on poetic psychology published three years ago in my *On English Poetry*" (which had been his B. Litt. thesis) to "*The Meaning of Dreams* which should be read as an introduction to the present volume" and is "a simply-written study of the mechanics of imaginative psychology." That said, Graves concludes with a qualified acceptance of the value of such analyses by defining his position as lying "between modern analytic psychology and the reading of poetry 'emotionally,' if you like, and 'for its own sake.'" In his rejection of Aristotelian rationality, Graves here extolled emotional thought combined with reading the poem "for its own sake," which I understand as reading the poem for its inescapable and essential reality: the kisses four or in "The Gnat" the sound of an insect lodged in the shepherd's ear. "The Gnat" first appeared in *The Pier-Glass* (1921) and was reprinted in *Poems (1914–1926).* Graves indicated in "Author's Note" to *Poetic Unreason* that "The Gnat" was of serious concern to him in *The Meaning of*

Dreams. After his discussion of the poem as a sign of his conflict between accepting ordinary employment and remaining a poet, Graves concluded that the gnat connects with his war neurosis by suggesting the "zero-hour of attack" and "the crazy noise of battle." And the last line expresses his concern that psychoanalysis might end his poetry (105).

If Graves had so ended his discussion of the poem, his adherence to translating illogical poetry and experience "into a more logical form" could be unquestioned. However, he ends the book ambiguously:

> But as a matter of fact, the logical interpretation of a not-logical poem does not in any way affect its value as a poem or even explain it altogether; as a poem it has a certain intense and not to be defined quality which must disappear in translation. The same is true about religious experiences; there is always a connection between these and the psychology that we have been studying here in the light of dreams; but to give an account of some variety of religious experience in terms of conflict between rival modes of behaviour, is not to give the experience itself. Between logical and not-logical experience there can be a close alliance; to set them at variance with greater preference for one than for the other is disastrous for both. (166–167)

Analyzed, the parts of this statement are:

> poems/dreams are not simply logical
> logical explanations are translations
> the experience itself is religious
> the logical and illogical must coexist.

Graves has become aware, as do all who live long enough, that experience differs greatly from any articulation of that experience: grief is different from mourning, the act of love is different from a love poem. The act may be unique and private, but the expression must be public and even conventional. Obviously troubled by this awareness, Graves held closely to the dream state, to the illogical as the source of poetry. What he only suggests is that he has had experiences, perhaps religious ones, that either resembled or occurred during the dream state. In 1924, though chary about discussing these experiences, they are the subject of the poetry he wrote after marriage. Never is his day-to-day life, in which he must be logical, the subject of poetry. Though he wrote drafts of poems on the back of chits from Nancy's store, he wrote no poems about being a storekeeper. The Graves who conducted the business of a writer was not the Graves who wrote the poems; and as he wrote, he could not allow those two to be in conflict. Such conflict would have either ended his life as poet or driven him completely mad. So he rendered unto each its due.

As Graves explained in his analysis of "The Gnat" in *The Meaning of Dreams,* he had become dependant on his neuroses as a source of poetry. The war, his marriage, his threadbare life as a poet were signs for him, and so similar to others, of an attempt to cope with a personality altered by the effects of World War I. And these neuroses may well have existed because that was an acceptable label for someone whose life and poetry expressed a willingness to be dominated, to be subject to, another person: his wife, his muse, and ultimately the Goddess. So many of the poems he wrote in the twenties repeat his understanding of his relationship with this composite feminine power that to pick one as illustrative is inviting: "A Valentine." The themes are, in general, common in Graves's love poetry from the twenties: hauntings, rejection, subservience. With such common themes, the poet yet is not celebrating a familiar experience. Instead, in pursuing the feminine, he pursues someone of "other shape and hue" who beckons him in "unfamiliar imagery." Graves would not publicly proclaim the historical presence and the significance of the Goddess and the Muse for years, but their roles certainly are compatible with the two female figures in "A Valentine": one human and familiar, the other unfamiliar, probably spiritual—"bright ghost."

Graves was no saint who would induce visions by going without food and water for a week and staying awake the whole time by tying his hair to the ceiling. Graves was a Romantic who found that one stimulus will arouse spirit, mind and body, as T. E. Hulme accurately summarized the nature of Romanticism, though he intended to condemn not describe:

> Romanticism, for example, confuses both human and divine things, by not clearly separating them. The main thing with which it can be reproached is that it blurs the clear outlines of human relations— whether in political thought or in the literary treatment of sex—by introducing in them the *Perfection* that properly belongs to the non-human. (10–11)

Though Graves would agree that a difference exists between "human" and "divine," he could not have accepted Hulme's rejection of the possibility of a mystical union. That union formed the basis of all Graves wrote. And

Hulme's rejection of the mystical indicates the difficulties Graves would have with the International Modernists and the scholars who have accepted their exclusionary discussions of modern poetry. Hulme's ideas in *Speculations* articulated the poetic belief of Pound et al. and became a programmatic definition of Modernist literature, with the implicit assertion that spirit and flesh cannot unite. Hence, love, patriotism, and mysticism are illusionary. Unfortunately, the manuscript of Hulme's study of heroism was lost when he was killed in World War I not long after he volunteered for service and not long after he was engaged to be married. If such an important voice had not been silenced, modern thought and literature might have developed with less divisiveness. The fervor of Hulme's attack on Romanticism indicates the importance he attributed to it as a literary and cultural force. Only critics writing after the fact have dismissed such importance, neglecting to note that such different poets as Graves and Eliot were viewed as equally significant by such an important exponent of "high modernism" as Virginia Woolf.

Graves's celebration in "A Valentine" is of the unfamiliar being who can neither be simply poetic inspiration, nor simply his familiar wife. That he might well have become aware of the spirit through his love of his wife is possible. More than likely he had, as Catherine Dalton wrote to me, actually experienced the Goddess. That he could have done so without the presence of Nancy Nicholson is unlikely. In healing him by substituting a domineering love for his fear of helplessness in battle, she opened the door into a spiritual reality that would obsess him and which he briefly acknowledged in "A History" (1924), that poem of the "death-white Fay." George Steiner, though meaning something entirely different, did indicate the essence of Graves's poetry when he wrote, "The highest intensities, the outermost splendors of language and emotion seem to lie beyond it" (349). Obviously, Steiner meant that Graves's poetry lacked such accomplishment, but what he may well be implying is that Graves's subject itself was beyond the talent of even the most accomplished of poets. Steiner read Graves with care.

By the time Graves wrote "A Valentine," he was no longer simply shaped by the language of Keats. He was shaped by the reality of Keats's poetry as well. The "dream-shape" he referred to as defining the Romantic poem has become as characteristic of Graves's poetry as of the Romantics'. Like them, he moved beyond metaphor and rhetoric into the reality of the spirit, but only in the most qualified sense did Graves accept the obligation Coleridge set for himself in the poems he contributed to *Lyrical Ballads:*

... it was agreed that my endeavors should be directed to persons and characters supernatural, or at least romantic; yet so as to transfer from our inward nature a human interest and a semblance of truth sufficient to procure for these shadows of imagination that willing suspension of disbelief for the moment, which constitutes poetic faith. (*Biographia Literaria* XIV)

There are poems, such as "Neglectful Edward" and "Loving Henry," in which Graves used the ballad to make his love and lover comprehensible. Even "The Pier-Glass" gives dramatic form to spirit. But the quick of his experience is not extrapolated or translated, but remains, as in "A Valentine," "unfamiliar." He probably did well to say no more than these are poems of "amatory fancy" which helped him through a painful war neurosis. In *My Head! My Head!* Graves explained through Elisha that when a seer or magician tells of the past, he is actually telling of the present. Later Graves explained his creation of past events in his historical fiction as the process of analeptic thinking. The past moves seamlessly into the present. In both explanations, visions—whether caused by the magician's present or his viewing the past—are parts of his immediate experience:

> What is past is past: it has been and it never can be again. A book spread out is not of the past nor of the future: it is the present. The history that it gives of anything that is past is not the past itself; it is the present. The forecast it makes of the future is not the future itself: it is the present. (MH 105)

By the mid-twenties, Graves had moved beyond theory and language about the spiritual world. Contact with it and the experience of it were essential to his life as poet.

Graves's poems of malevolent female spirits certainly have, for him, familiar precedent in such poems as Coleridge's "Christabel" and Keats's "Lamia," as well as the ever popular Gothic. That Graves wished to find a readership is clear, so he may have turned his hand to such tales. Without doubt, Graves would have been aware of such popularity and not, then, turned from it because of its popularity. He has indicated that he wrote with an eye to his audience as with the poem about old Adelphine and even *Good-Bye To All That*. He had chosen his occupation: writer. Yet he could have stayed with war poetry and nursery rhymes, both successful for him and both assured of readers. That he did not, I have related to his process of dealing with his war neurosis: he invested Nancy Nicholson with complete responsibility for his life and would live or die as she wished. As in "A Valentine," his submission seems more personal than rhetorical, more the statement of his own dependence than that of the traditional lover pining for lost love. Graves had not lost love. Instead, he was stating the terms he had accepted. Later he would proclaim such authority as endemic to the White Goddess, and his movement from a psychological to an historical understanding of the power of woman is, probably, the single most important event in his spiritual and artistic life. Most likely that event occurred during the writing of the poems in *Mock Beggar Hall*. Published in 1924, a year after *The Feather Bed*, *Mock Beggar Hall* marks Graves's departure from poetry with a grounding in psychology.

Though Graves published *The Meaning of Dreams* in 1925 and *Poetic Unreason* in 1925, both continuations of his interest in psychology, they originated much earlier. Both seem written with an eye for a popular audience. *The Meaning of Dreams* is Graves's development of Rivers's ideas about dream and poetry, and *Poetic Unreason* is Graves's development of his B. Litt. thesis, "The Illogical Element in English Poetry." In "Author's Note" to *Poetic Unreason*," he explained that the book had been "sitting on my shoulders like a Proteus constantly changing shape." It had undergone nine revisions and had been interrupted by two other books, *Mock Beggar Hall*, which provided the "poetic and philosophic background," and *The Meaning of Dreams*, which was intended as an introduction to *Poetic Unreason* and provided "a simply-written study of the mechanics of imaginative psychology." By "imaginative psychology," Graves meant the psychology of the imagination, a study of the unconscious, which had been his first entry to a reality he could call non-rational, one that could be expressed in the non-Aristotelian mode that had become so important to him.

In time he would definitively reject depth psychology, as he did the teaching of Freud and Jung by the time he wrote *The Meaning of Dreams*. There is, in fact, ample evidence in *Poetic Unreason* to posit the view that he had great difficulty in accepting the psychological origins of poetry and did not accept any theory of archetypes discoverable in the personal or collective unconscious. For he discusses the war trauma of a man confronted in his dreams by a threatening cat as "a historical experience" (147), not as a dream arising from previously existing images in the unconscious. As a child, the man had actually experienced a situation in which retreat to safety was blocked by a cat, so when during the war a dummy hand grenade was tossed into his dugout, blocking his escape, he related the emotions to an already existing image: the cat. The experience in the poem "A Child's Nursery Nightmare" is so close to his discussion of the traumatized soldier that to identify the officer with Graves makes sense. Also, relating war to nursery by means of analogy is basic to Graves's poetic at the time. He has other views of how a poem could develop from trauma, but never does he indicate that contact with the creatures of the unconscious is one. History and experience have become his principal sources. What remains from his earlier theories is a reliance on non-rational thought.

He will never abandon this reliance, and in *The White Goddess* Graves will discuss how even a physician can diagnose without recourse to rational thought, after which he concluded that "all original discoveries and inventions and musical and poetical compositions are the result of proleptic thought—the anticipation, by means of a suspension of time, of a result that could not have been arrived at by inductive reasoning—and of what may be called analeptic thought, the recovery of lost events by the same suspension" (280). Perhaps if Graves had corresponded with Jung, he would have found him receptive to the idea that the divinities informing the poet exist as part of the experienced world, not only as shards of a racial memory.

Edward Marsh did not understand some poems intended for *Whipperginny*. Graves explained to him that they were written for a time in the future when understanding "morbid psychology" would be commonplace. Graves also relegated some of the offending poems to the small book *The Feather Bed*. This period in his development as a poet remained important to Graves. He reflected on it in *Good-Bye To All That* as if it were ancient history, not merely what he had written just before the arrival of Laura Riding. Recalling that he wrote without concern for "the ordinary reading public" and did not think in terms of obligations of posterity, Graves claimed he wrote "only when and because there was a poem pressing to be written." Probably with reference to Marsh's rejection of the poems in *Whipperginny*, Graves observed that he had been "accused of trying to get publicity and increase" his sales with a "willful and clowning modernism." In his own view, he was simply exercising "greater strictness" in his writings and using the knowledge of his "new psychological studies" that first appeared in *Whipperginny* (GBTAT 292). In fact, Graves had written out of a very similar psychological paradigm in both *Country Sentiment* and *The Pier-Glass*, one which regarded association rather than reason as the structure of a poem, and the conflicts in the unconscious as the source of images and symbols.

The most obvious connections between the poems and psychology are the absence of reality restrained by propriety and the self-consciousness of Frazer's discussions of primitive culture. Graves would have looked with favor on Frazer's writings not only because they separated him from the simple faith of his Victorian childhood, but because Rivers had also looked closely at primitive rituals. The connections between these rituals and the world of the unconscious were accepted as readily by Graves as by T. S. Eliot. Graves could have echoed Eliot's note to *The Waste Land* stating his indebtedness to *The Golden Bough*, "which has influenced our generation profoundly" (147). Referring to a "clowning modernism," Graves may well have been thinking of "The Snake and the Bull," a playful poem about totems and jungle gods, which John Vickery saw as Graves's merging the discoveries of depth psychology and Frazer (16–20).

Of even more startling effect is Graves's attack on the traditional reality of both Victorians and Catholics in "The Feather Bed." His approach to Catholics is very like Protestant nun-baiting as he ascribes lesbian longings to a Mother Superior. His rejection of Victorian influence is more understandable since he wished to be free of a world cloistered by little taste and less tolerance. The poem continues to castigate Victorians for attacks on Darwin and Gladstone with the only links being strongly associative, too much so for Marsh, and troubling enough to Graves that he explained the poems in an "Introductory Letter To John Ransome" as "a study of a fatigued mind in a fatigued body and under the stress of an abnormal conflict" (FB 5). This caveat is inadequate to justify Graves's closely reasoned argument, which dismisses "Jehovah, the God of the present, predominately male, violent, blundering, deceitful, with great insistence on uniformity of rites, duties and taboos, at whatever cost to the individual" and proclaims the coming to power of "Lucifer, the God of the future," who will promulgate a "doctrine of mutual responsibility for error, and of mutual respect between individuals, sexes, classes, groups, and nations, a higher conception than the eye for an eye and tooth for a tooth doctrine of Jehovah" (FB 7). Though some of these views can be attributed to Nancy Nicholson, more likely Graves was writing for the modern intellectuals gathered around the Morrells and the Woolfs. And then *The Waste Land* had been published in 1922. Its notoriety would not have escaped Graves, nor would the significance it established for both psychology and myth. Graves and Eliot were close in their rejection of the Victorian reality. Only the interference of Laura Riding caused a rift between the two. Beryl Graves told me when we talked in May of 1999 that Graves was very pleased when he resumed his friendship with Eliot, who published *The White Goddess* at Faber after two other houses had rejected it.

Nancy's efforts to heal Graves's war trauma by providing an obsessive and tyrannical love must have been difficult for both, but provided the main mooring for Graves, holding his widely associative thoughts in check. And clearly the conflicts were "abnormal," as he wrote in his dedicatory letter to *The Feather Bed*. Such a modern and iconoclastic work would have appealed to its publishers, Leonard and Virginia Woolf, though I imagine their understanding of Graves's next volume, *Mock Beggar Hall*, was more conventional.

Graves's poems in *Mock Beggar Hall* evoke both the intellectual and physical environment of Oxford. The Woolfs were part of Lady Ottoline Morrell's group of intellectuals and pacifists who met often at Garsington, the Morrells' home, as was Graves, though he first met the Woolfs when he stopped by unannounced. His invitation to Garsington came through Siegfried Sassoon, who would have been introduced to Lady Ottoline Morrell by her friend and lover, Bertrand Russell, who orchestrated Sassoon's pacifist gesture. The books Graves published with Hogarth would have appealed both to the Woolfs' modern intellectuality and their pacifist sympathies, though these were not books Graves expected to profit from financially, as he indicated to his agent, Pinker, advising him in a letter of 25 March 1925 to be certain to retain copyright for a later collection of essays (UTHRC). His reasons for publishing with Hogarth were probably to put himself as poet among the "obvious names," since he did not aspire to be part of their social set. "Interchange of Selves" and "Mock Beggar Hall" are both dialogues based on Graves's friendship with Basanta Mallik, the Indian political philosopher. The intellectual pacifism would have appealed to the Woolfs. Graves's beast fables, such as "Attercop: The All-Wise Spider," and poems based on classical reading, such as "Hemlock," a supposed translation of a "late-Greek satire," indicate the similar educations of Victorians of the privileged classes. His pacifist attitudes and his interest in psychology made him compatible with other authors they published: Roger Fry, T. S. Eliot, Bonamy Dobree, E. M. Forster, the Woolfs themselves. Yet Graves seldom departed from his comfortable rhyming poetry. Accommodating Hogarth, he also held to his own traditions. And he did not continue the views that made him attractive to the Woolfs, as he explained in his "Argument," which introduced the novel *My Head! My Head!*:

This introduction is an amplification and in part a retreat from what I wrote three years ago as a preface to my poem The Feather Bed: *I was then still to a certain extent attached to the individualist claim, look-*

*ing on Lucifer with warmth as a champion of Peace and on Moses
with hatred as a bloody-minded charlatan.* (24)

Graves attributed Isaac Rosenberg's play *Moses* with making his own
view "more generous." He came to see Moses as a leader who inspired a
"sense of heroic strength," a man to be remembered as a *"heroic deliverer
rather than as a narrow-minded unpitying upholder of* Law and Order"
(24–25). Graves's capitulation of adherence to the right and virtue of an
independent (even anarchic) moral or political stand was, actually, only
the renouncing of a briefly held view. Graves who managed Sassoon's
Medical Board and Graves who described himself to Marsh as a confirmed "militarist" was not likely to view the rebellious Lucifer as heroic.
Nor was he likely to consider Russell and the other conscientious objec-
tors as heroic. After his recess among the intellectual pacifists, he never
again made gestures in agreement with such views. Perhaps his war neuroses influenced him when he had his sojourn. But of more significance
would be his friendship with militarists such as John Buchan, Edward
Marsh, and T. E. Lawrence, to whom he dedicated *My Head! My Head!*
Graves named both Buchan and Lawrence as well as the Earl of Oxford,
the Vice Chancellor of Oxford, and the Poet Laureate when he wrote
Marsh on 20 October 1925 asking Marsh to assist him in his application
at the Royal University in Cairo: "The appointment is a Foreign Office
one. If you know any of the people there & get a chance would you reas-
sure them if they have any doubts as to my capacity and ability to be on
good behavior in an executive job."

Virginia Woolf was writing *Mrs. Dalloway* during the time she published Graves and may well have been intrigued by Graves's so evident
symptoms of shell shock. Neither she nor Graves suggests a meeting other
than the one recorded in her diary on 27 April 1925, by which time
Mrs. Dalloway was in print. Yet Septimus and Graves closely resemble
each other in their response to noise. The most common of noises can
panic them. Though neither Graves nor Septimus "recovered" from their
war trauma, Graves did live a long life, accepting as he did that fear and
awe were basic to his existence. Graves did not remain in the limbo of a
debilitating neurosis, but ascended to view the Goddess herself. He would
spend his life annotating the history of her power. *Mock Beggar Hall* contains early examples of this historical approach. What is unusual in the
volume is the poem "Witches," which he asserts was based on *A True
Discourse of the Apprehension of Sundry Witches lately taken in Scotland*
(*1591*)(MBH 24). Graves, of course, was fond of writing poetry and fic-

tion based on historical events, but his choosing to present the appearance of witches as historical led him to censure those who limit reality to the mundane, and to proclaim the existence of a spiritual world. After describing the flight of the witches "Wedgewise by thirteens," he dismisses those who have not so traveled, suggesting that he had:

> Do you, my cribbed empiricist,
> Judge these things false, then false they'll be
> For all who never swooped and kissed
> Above the mood, below the sea;
> Yet set no tangles in their place
> Of Time and Space and Gravity. (23)

Though Graves, even in his youth, was widely and deeply learned, he had not before suggested a familiarity with the spirit world—beyond hauntings and the visits of succubi and incubi. He would, though, in *My Head! My Head!* give fictive evidence of the power of the occult, and he would indicate how the passing of the magician's power from person to person occurred as he told of Elijah's coming upon the young Elisha as the latter plowed his father's fields:

> As the plough team went by he twitched his mantle for a moment across the shoulders of Elisha, and then, uncovering his appearance plainly from the cloak of thought, turned his back and went away across the furrows. Elisha understood what it was that the prophet intended. He halted his team and with an ox-goad still held in his hand hastened after Elijah. He cried, "Man of God, since you have summoned me, I shall follow you; but first let me kiss my father and my mother and let me offer a sacrifice." (32)

Remembering Elisha's explanation that the past lives in the present, I see Graves here telling of his own present life through the story of Elisha and the Shunamite woman, his stated concern. Yet this novel figures largely in the story told here of Graves's creative life, which no later than 1924 became informed by his spiritual life, a life lived within the occult experience of spirits who can be evoked and who can touch both the quick and the dead. In "Witches," Graves reveals knowledge and interest in the occult, an interest that would eventually result in *The White Goddess*. Both works affirm a historical truth, not a psychological condition. Graves would not again credit depth psychology with leading him to truth.

Graves would suggest a new course in *The Marmosite's Miscellany,* published by Hogarth in 1925. In this caustic and contemporary poem, Graves seems determined to find a place in the front ranks of modern poets. He would use his familiar beast fable to praise his intellectual idol, Samuel Butler, and mildly satirize his successful and senior contemporaries: Masefield, Bennett, Davies, and Shaw. As Martin Seymour-Smith observed, the gentle satire of the poem did not draw blood and seemed rather intended as Graves's statement of separation from any poetic school (119). Graves would reiterate his desire to be free of schools in *Contemporary Techniques of Poetry,* which Hogarth would also publish in 1925. In this cleverly structured study, Graves treats poetic schools as analogous to political parties: Left Wing to Liberal and Right Wing to Conservative, with nodding acknowledgment of Communist, Labour, and Independent adherents. He himself resembles what he likes best: the "Central or Liberal" poetry of the Georgians that had been "popularly accepted as fairly representing all that is most hopeful in the poetry of this age" (10). He would excoriate Georgianism as backward in *A Survey of Modernist Poetry,* indicating the influence of Riding. But in the year before he actually met her, he found many virtues in his first poetic home, especially their "self-imposed limits" in diction, meter, and rhyme. He found comfortable their whole-hearted approval of rhyme for instance. His sympathy was with the Left Wing when he discussed the essential content of poetry, especially "the predominance of this fantastic dream structure in Left-Wing poetry." He read this as a challenge to the "practical man," the man of the Right Wing who might allow dream as a rhetorical device but would reject the practical life confusedly mixed up with dream:

> The Right Wing regards this as madness, for the definition of insanity is that the insane does not distinguish dreaming from waking. But the Left Wing does not value the practical life more than the dream, and often a good deal less. The political analogy here is easy and important. (CTP 46–47)

The "political analogy" is to the poets with a reality firmly based in the solid public reality of the Victorians, in contrast with the reality of those who had their psyches shaken and often destroyed by World War I, between those who held to Aristotelian thought and those who didn't. And more to the point, Graves could have distinguished between those who can limit the spiritual to the church and those whose lives have been invaded by a spiritual (or psychological) reality they cannot control. And to the point, Graves neither could nor wished to "distinguish dreaming from waking." As he knew, and as Catherine Dalton wrote to me, he would have been considered mad if he had written of his experience of the divinity he called "the death-white Fay."

In general, Graves makes his distinctions without rancor and often groups together poets whom later, and less tolerant, critics find so disparate that they would not include them in the same discussion. Among the poets of the Left, Laura Riding ominously appears, represented by "The Quids," which Graves describes as "a satire on traditional metaphysics; and a first favourite with me" (CTP 19). As poets "committed to revolution," he lists: T. S. Eliot, Osbert and Sacherval Sitwell, Ford Maddox Hueffer as "the doyen of the party," Siegfried Sassoon. Among the Independents, "standing somewhere between Centre and Left" is Lascelles Abercrombie, who "has given more thought to the fundamentals of poetic technique than any other living Englishman" (CTP 12). Graves, as well as others, at the time considered that the living poets were engaged in the same act from different perspectives, but they were not members of different species and, certainly, were not more or less worthy of the name "poet" because of their beliefs and practices.

Contemporary Techniques of Poetry is an important touchstone for several reasons. It allowed Graves to separate himself formally from all camps, which he had not done in earlier studies in which he regularly discussed his own poetry; it served as the paradigm for most of his later studies, in which personal friendship is more important than the poet's camp; and it indicated the state of poetry in the twenties in that it cut across the lines of class and was published under the imprimatur of the Woolfs at Hogarth. And it did, of course, signal the end of critical balance in Graves for the next fifteen years. After the advent of Laura Riding in 1926, Graves had a willing collaborator in his new turn to contemporary intellectuality and would write prose that sounded more like T. S. Eliot's than his own earlier writings. He no longer used his own poems, as he did with "The Gnat," to illustrate his ideas, but wrote, as in *The Marmosite's Miscellany,* as a distanced critic—an inspector of the passing poetic scene. In *A Survey of Modernist Poetry,* which he wrote with Riding, they would reject Graves's earlier view that the poem reveals the "essential" character of the poet for a much more fashionable stance in describing the modernist poet, a poet separate from "dead" movements. The "personality" of the poem is "its quality of independence from both the reader and the poet," making it "a new and self-explanatory creature," different from the personality of the poet (124).

Graves needed independence from the forces that had shaped him and was acquiring it before he met Riding. She, however, appeared at a most useful moment, though one that was personally stressful to the Graves family. She and Robert Graves separated themselves from propriety, but not from association with the influential. Friendships with Sassoon and Marsh continued. And it was Gertrude Stein who suggested Mallorca to them; they would later separate angrily because of Stein's rejection of Riding. His friendship with Edith Sitwell also ended when Laura Riding became a factor in his life. As Seymour-Smith records, she had given and inscribed to Robert and Nancy a copy of *The Sleeping Beauty*, which he sold in 1926 to raise money to support his bohemian life. Sitwell bought back the book and under her original inscription, which read, "For Robert Graves and Nancy Nicholson in admiration from Edith Sitwell," she wrote:

> I wrote this dedication at a time when Robert Graves was still a tentative English nightingale and not an American loon or screech-owl. Though poor, I am happy to buy this book (from the shop to which he sold it) for the sum of 15s so that no one can accuse me of being a hoot-fan. (136–137)

Few of Graves's friends and peers regarded his association with Laura Riding as positive. But then, too, they regarded him as a defier of convention. And they were right, for Graves would pursue his own course. Neither traditional Georgian nor conventional Modernist, Graves had paid with a reputation too small to fit his genius and talent. To credit Laura Riding with effecting his defection not only from propriety but also from poetic camps is to overvalue her role. Graves had accomplished both before her arrival, yet her presence made his decisions public. Though more than a rhetorical convention, Laura Riding did not create Robert Graves, the poet. She midwifed a role he played in the public's eyes, as had Nancy with her shop. When he had stepped from the everyday, even the everyday of his war neuroses, into the fabulous, he fashioned a poetic and a creative life that would make simple classification impossible.

It would seem that *The Marmosite's Miscellany* had set Graves on a new path, that of the fashionable and removed intellectual. Such was not the case. Graves would always be aware that with his wounding in the war, he had left part of his reality and accepted much that was new, unfamiliar and unreasonable. Or to be affirmative: he entered a world in which the miraculous could appear—and could overwhelm his sanity, as he wrote in "The Cool Web," the last poem in *Poems (1914–1926):*

Children are dumb to say how hot the day is,
How hot the scent of the summer rose,
How dreadful the black wastes of evening sky,
How dreadful the tall soldiers drumming by.

But we have speech that cools the hottest sun,
And speech that dulls the hottest rose's scent.
We spell away the overhanging night,
We spell away the soldiers and the fright.

There's a cool web of language winds us in,
Retreat from too much gladness, too much fear:
We grow sea-green at last and coldly die
In brininess and volubility.

But if we let our tongues lose self-possession,
Throwing off language and its wateriness
Before our death, instead of when death comes,
Facing the brightness of the children's day,
Facing the rose, the dark sky, and the drums,
We shall go mad no doubt and die that way. (215–216)

He ends the volume by evoking his dominant concerns over the past ten years: the damage done by war, children's fears, the paradox of love, and the possibility of madness. He would not write a more complex and self-revelatory poem, nor one that would place him more securely within the poetic concerns of his time. Here is Eliot's Prufrock, troubled lest "human voices wake us and we drown," and Yeats, troubled by the "rose's cruel scent." Though Graves may well have been echoing these poems, "The Cool Web" is his own. His experiences must have seemed, even to him, those of a lunatic, one driven mad by the moon—the Goddess's own sign. In his writing, the unreasonable and implausible found life. Contradictory and frightening, his visionary poetry did hold him from madness—almost to the end of his life. Unfortunately, language deserted him before he died. What he heard in his head, no one will ever know. Indeed, we may never know what he saw and called "the death-white Fay."

AFTERWORD

Graves had been a 'Georgian' and later in his *Poetic Unreason* and other critical essays had set a fashion in psychological analysis of the effect on readers of various poetic devices. He was now declaring the intrinsic truth of his statements rather than their probable appeal to anthology readers.

Robert Graves and Alan Hodge, *The Long Week-End*

Graves and Hodge first published their social history of England between the wars in 1940, when the relationship between Graves and Riding was gone but not forgotten. Graves placed Riding and her views highly in this study: that it was important to strive for non-historical truth and reject work that was merely a popular success. Graves's confrontation with W. B. Yeats for not including Riding in *The Oxford Book of Modern Poetry* was phrased as Graves's opposition to "anthologies." As he mentioned in replying to Yeats, he and Riding had made their position clear in *A Pamphlet Against Anthologies*. Riding's opposition to anthologies perhaps turned upon a lack of invitations. Though Graves and Riding staunchly objected to merely popular literature, Graves continued to write prose, fiction, and nonfiction that was popular and financially successful. He had begun his career with studies of poetry and established his credentials with historical novels and his autobiography. The money was important because he had a family to support—and Laura Riding, who was not a low-maintenance being. He had made several continuations of his popular success: sequels to novels, a play with the title *But It Still Goes On*. And of course, he had a growing reputation as a poet. And with the end of his relationship with Riding, he and Beryl Hodge would start a family. Fortunately, the second family coincided with the period of Graves's greatest success, not only financial but literary. His fame spread, and Deya became a magnetic field attracting writers of great significance as well as devotees, such as me.

The most important literary event in Graves's life as writer would occur in 1944 when he interrupted his work on the novel *The Golden Fleece* to write, in a few weeks, the first draft of *The White Goddess*. With the writing of this book, Graves proclaimed the study and celebration of the Goddess to be his one theme, his guiding passion. She had, however, been present in his writing, especially poetry, for years. And even before she appeared, Graves had sensed her form in the healing power of his wife. Graves's method, as well as what he wrote, is important.

In writing *The White Goddess*, Graves followed the non-rational method he had come to call "analeptic." As with the method described in *Poetic Unreason* and *The Meaning of Dreams*, the analeptic method did not rely on logically arrived-at understanding. Instead, Graves immersed himself in primary texts until he no longer felt a separation between himself and the material. However, as he tells the tale of being inspired to write *The White Goddess*, he had no previous understanding of the poems of Taliesin that are central to his understanding of the Goddess. He had been working with Greek materials and admiralty charts concerning the voyage of Jason. And the White Goddess, of Graves's book, is Celtic. So the ideas came to Graves, actually, as they had in the past, from inherited or intuitive understanding. He was always fortunate in that he enjoyed the company of people who could clarify or corroborate his perceptions. Nancy Nicholson had led him to channel his neurasthenia, at least to the point that he could exist with his hauntings. Laura Riding is reflected in the mercilessly analytical Livia of the Claudius novels, who was as harshly critical of Claudius as Riding was of Graves. Beryl Hodge provided for Graves care and protection, as well as firm guidance. These three women share the authority Graves the writer needed.

Although Graves does not acknowledge his debt to his father, another fortuitous being in Graves's career, he owed much to him. Alfred Perceval Graves had been president of the Irish Literary Society, editor of *Every Irishman's Library*, and a scholar of Irish folk songs. His son would have grown up with the bardic tradition strongly imprinted on him. What he did in *The White Goddess* was to make the traditional Irish and Welsh poetry turn upon praise of the Goddess. The traditional poet, or ollave, was mainly concerned with expressing a "complex poetic truth" in clear and exacting statements. Though devoted to praising "Brigid, the Threefold Muse," his erudite education in history, music, law, science, and divination did at times cause him to fall under the spell of "Ogma the god of

Eloquence." This was likely to occur when he was engaged in exchanges of wit and poetry with his colleagues, fellow poets, the only people whose judgment mattered to him. In medieval Wales the court poet had almost completely "forgotten the theme" and wrote only for profit, which was denied the minstrel, who evidenced the "greater poetic integrity" (19). Though he was true to the theme himself, Graves did change the terms of his understanding of it, a change well illustrated by his revision of this poem, titled "In Dedication":

> Your broad, high brow is whiter than a leper's,
> Your eyes are flax-flower blue, blood-red your lips,
> Your hair curls honey-coloured to white hips.
>
> All saints revile you, and all sober men
> ruled by the God Apollo's golden mean;
> Yet for me rises even in November
> (Rawest of month) so cruelly new a vision,
> Cerridwen, of your beatific love
> I forget violence and long betrayal,
> Careless of where the next bright bolt may fall. (v)

In revising the poem, as well as striking a much more literary and less immediate note, Graves changed two words and in so doing separated this portrait of the Goddess from the one that had so terrified him earlier. Her lips changed from "blood-red" to "rowan-berry," and her "violence" became merely "cruelty" (3). Though the changes are small, like the buzzing sounds in "The Gnat," the earlier are straws that can break a poet's back. The Goddess of the first version belongs to Graves in the twenties, during that time of terror tainted always by a violence he was struggling to accept as a permanent part of his existence. That he would distance himself from its presence is humanly understandable. Too much familiarity breeds madness.

Though Graves had his personal and poetic past to instruct him, his perceptions exceeded his understanding, especially of Celtic culture. But Graves was a talented, even inspired, researcher—though he would probably not accept the designation. That Graves did not know the Celtic languages was, of course, a limitation. But he was again fortunate in his acquaintances. In a long correspondence with Valentin Iremonger, Graves confirmed and amplified his understanding. Although Iremonger's letters to Graves do not seem to be extant, Graves's letters are in the possession of Sheila Iremonger, widow of Valentin—a poet and a diplomat. Largely, Iremonger confirmed Graves's research, though he did provide translations from the Irish as well. Iremonger appeared pleased to be of help to a fellow poet, a response compatible with Graves's own understanding of the proper relationship among poets. Memory is quite Irish in Graves, who never forgot such friends as Frost and cummings, and never forgave Pound.

My interest in Irish poetry led me to write Graves to ask him how he felt about being called "the last of the Anglo-Irish poets" by James Liddy, editor of the Irish literary journal *Arena* (4:1). Liddy also published Graves's poem "Dynamite Barbee" in spring 1965, the last issue. Though *Arena* had been deservedly reprinted in 1981, "Dynamite Barbee" did not become a part of Graves's oeuvre. He did not reprint this poem, a wise decision not only because of its lack of merit, but also because it was copyrighted by International Authors S.A. Several writers, including Graves and Graham Greene, were pulled into a financial and literary management deal that collapsed, leaving the clients out of royalties. Unfortunately, Graves had works of more literary and financial value in their hands.

Perhaps Liddy was thinking of the wild streak in the Anglo-Irish when he wrote his introduction to "Dynamite Barbee." But Graves's response on Easter Sunday 1969 to my query is by far more appropriate to the literary Anglo-Irish than the poem:

> Am I the last of the Anglo-Irish poets? Well maybe. Our family went to Ireland in 1575 and I still retain the family's respect for "English as they speak it in Ireland." Which means with correctitude and love.

Edith Sitwell observed that after meeting Riding, Graves lost his song and became shrill and American. Sitwell was excessive at the time. More accurately, when Graves wrote outside his own tradition, he sounded like a parody of his adopted tradition. In the case of "Dynamite Barbee," his Americanisms are the equivalent of the stage Irish of film: excessive and stylized, as this stanza shows:

> Sunk to the bottom, we guessed she would:
> Three times down and she's gone for good.
> Dynamite Barbee, no! Man, no! (71)

Graves wrote with knowledge and verve on a variety of cultures and religions: Hebrew, Christian, Islamic, as well as those of ancient Greece and

Rome. Yet his voice, especially in poetry, remained that of an Englishman of his class and time who had come to delight in his own nature, as in "Flying Crooked":

The butterfly, a cabbage-white,
(His honest idiocy of flight)
Will never now, it is too late,
Master the art of flying straight,
Yet has—who knows so well as I?—
A just sense of how not to fly;
He lurches here and here by guess
And God and hope and hopelessness.
Even the acrobatic swift
Has not his flying-crooked gift. (NMG 45)

"Flying Crooked" was first published in *Poems 1926–1930*, after Graves had moved to Mallorca. Yet he chose the homey cabbage-white rather than an exotic butterfly native to the Mediterranean to carry the image of his own idiosyncratic talent that moved compulsively through time and place, all the while remaining English.

Even his description of the Goddess comes from traditions seated in the British Isles, though they are Celtic. In "The White Goddess" (WG, chapter 4), Graves made clear that she is universally manifest, with the "most comprehensive and inspired account of the Goddess in all ancient literature" in Apuleius's *Golden Ass*. Graves chose to quote from a translation by William Adlington, "where Lucius invokes her from the depth of misery and spiritual degradation" (65):

About the first watch of the night when I had slept my first sleep, I awakened with sudden fear and saw the moon shining bright as when she is at the full and seeming as though she leaped out of the sea. (65–66)

For Lucius, as for Graves, the fear inspired by the moon becomes awe. The Goddess is invoked and appears, explaining that she has been called by many names, her own true name being Queen Isis. As was Graves, Lucius was saved from terror and death by the intervention of the Goddess, and in his own translation of *The Golden Ass*, Graves echoed his early poem "I Hate The Moon." Lucius has fallen into a "sweet, sound sleep":

> Not long afterwards I awoke in sudden terror. A dazzling full moon was rising from the sea. It is at this secret hour that the Moon-goddess, sole sovereign of mankind, is possessed of her greatest power and majesty. She is the shining deity by whose divine brilliance not only all beasts, wild and tame, but all inanimate things as well, are invigorated; whose ebbs and flows control the rhythm of all bodies whatever, whether in the air, on earth, or below the sea. (236)

Graves has taken care to translate the experiences of Lucius as he took care to document the manifestations of the Goddess. And no reader need stretch belief to see the salvation of Lucius in the salvation of Graves. Both were saved by the intervention of women who assumed complete and ir-revocable power over their lives.

Graves does not intimate that Apuleius was only writing of a fictional character or of a figure of speech such as Jung's anima. In our skeptical and still-Aristotelian age, divine beings and their prophets have been rele-gated to history or perhaps to legend. In "A History" (1924) Graves wrote of actually being in the presence of the Goddess, and I believe he knew her, not metaphorically, but actually. Very early, Graves's poetic conventions could not express the reality he called "unfamiliar" in "A Valentine" (1923) and he would spend his life searching history and literature for her biography. In his writings, he would never be completely successful in de-scribing his experience of the divine, for the mystical experience must be unique, unfamiliar in a commonplace world. Yet to accept that Graves's experience of the Goddess actually occurred changes the way in which he must be read. He abandoned conventions and schools as they failed to meet his needs, holding always to his one story. More of my questions are answered by accepting the simple fact that the Goddess appeared to Rob-ert Graves. I believe she did, just as I believed him when he picked up a curved dagger in a silver scabbard from Afghanistan and said: "There are only thirty-three of these in the world. And only the sons of the prophet have them. That is why I have this one" (*Conversations* 74). Yet Graves never presumed to be more than poet. When I asked Beryl Graves about his concern with magic, she simply handed me the poem "At Best, Poets":

> Woman with her forests, moons, flowers, waters,
> And watchful fingers:
> We claim no magic comparable to hers—
> At best poets; at worst, sorcerers. (10)

WORKS CITED

Abbreviations Used in the Text

Works by Robert Graves

BCNYPL	Berg Collection, New York Public Library
CP 1	*Complete Poems*, vol. 1
CP 2	*Complete Poems*, vol. 2
CP 3	*Complete Poems*, vol. 3
CS	*Country Sentiment*
CTP	*Contemporary Techniques of Poetry*
DQEA	*Difficult Questions, Easy Answers*
FB	*The Feather Bed*
FF	*Fairies and Fusiliers*
GBTAT	*Good-Bye To All That*
GD	*Goliath and David*
MBH	*Mock Beggar Hall*
MD	*The Meaning of Dreams*
MH	*My Head! My Head!*
MM	*The Marmosite's Miscellany*
OB	*Over the Brazier*
OEP	*On English Poetry*
PG	*The Pier-Glass*
PU	*Poetic Unreason and Other Studies*
SMP	*A Survey of Modernist Poetry*
TB	*Treasure Box*
UTHRC	University of Texas at Austin, Harry Ransom Humanities Research Center
WG	*The White Goddess*

Works by Siegfried Sassoon

CPSS   *Collected Poems of Siegfried Sassoon*
CMOGS   *Complete Memoirs of George Sherston*

Aldington, Richard. *Lawrence of Arabia: A Biographical Enquiry*. London: Collins,
    1955.
Auden, W. H. *Selected Poems*. Edited by Edward Mendelson. London: Faber, 1979.
Brooke, Rupert. *The Poetical Works of Rupert Brooke*. Edited by Geoffrey Keynes.
    London: Faber and Faber, 1977.
Buchan, John. *The Four Adventures of Richard Hannay*. Introduction by Robin W.
    Winks. Boston: David R. Godine, 1988.
Coleridge, Samuel Taylor. *Biographia Literaria*. London: George Bell and Sons, 1905.
Dalton (Graves), Catherine. Letters to Frank Kersnowski dated 26 October and
    31 October 1997.
Davie, Donald. "Impersonal and Emblematic." *Shenandoah* 13 (winter 1962): 38–
    44.
Durrell, Lawrence. *Quinx, or The Ripper's Tale*. London: Faber and Faber, 1985.
Eliot, Thomas Stearns. *Collected Poems, 1909–1962*. New York: Harcourt Brace,
    1968.
———. *The Waste Land. A Facsimile and Transcript of the Original Drafts Including
    the Annotations of Ezra Pound*. Edited by Valerie Eliot. New York: Harcourt
    Brace Jovanovich, 1971.
Frazer, James George. *The Golden Bough*. Abridged edition. London: Macmillan,
    1922.
Freud, Sigmund. *The Interpretation of Dreams*. New York: Avon, 1965.
Frost, Robert. *Complete Poems of Robert Frost*. New York: Holt, Rinehart and Win-
    ston, 1964.
Fussell, Paul. *The Great War and Modern Memory*. New York and London: Oxford,
    1975.
Graves, Alfred Perceval. *To Return To All That*. London: Jonathan Cape, 1930.
Graves, Beryl. Letter to Frank Kersnowski dated 7 June 1998.
Graves, Richard Perceval. *Robert Graves: The Assault Heroic, 1895–1926*. London:
    Weidenfeld and Nicholson, 1986.
Graves, Robert. *An Ancient Castle*. Illustrated by Elizabeth Graves. With an after-
    word by William David Thomas. New York: Michael Kesend Publishing, 1981.
———. *Another Future of Poetry*. London: Hogarth Press, 1926.
———. "Children of Darkness" manuscripts. Poetry and Rare Book Collection, State
    University of New York at Buffalo.
———. *Collected Poems*. Garden City, N.Y.: Doubleday and Company, 1961.
———. *Collected Poems*. London: Cassell, 1975.
———. *Complete Poems*. Volume 1. Edited by Beryl Graves and Dunstan Ward.
    Manchester: Carcanet; Paris: Alyscamps, 1995.
———. *Complete Poems*. Volume 2. Edited by Beryl Graves and Dunstan Ward.
    Manchester: Carcanet; Paris: Alyscamps, 1997.

———. *Complete Poems.* Volume 3. Edited by Beryl Graves and Dunstan Ward. Manchester: Carcanet; Paris: Alyscamps, 1999.

———. *Complete Short Stories.* Edited by Lucia Graves. Manchester: Carcanet; Paris: Alyscamps, 1995.

———. *Contemporary Techniques of Poetry.* London: Hogarth Press, 1925.

———. *Conversations with Robert Graves.* Edited, with an introduction, by Frank Kersnowski. Jackson: University Press of Mississippi, 1989.

———. *Country Sentiment.* New York: Alfred Knopf, 1920.

———. *Difficult Questions, Easy Answers.* Garden City, N.Y.: Doubleday, 1973.

———. *Fairies and Fusiliers.* New York: Alfred Knopf, 1918.

———. *The Feather Bed.* London: Hogarth Press, 1923.

———. *Five Pens in Hand.* Freeport: Books for Libraries, 1970.

———. *Goliath and David.* London: Chiswick Press, 1916.

———. *Good-Bye To All That: An Autobiography.* Edited, with a biographical essay and annotations, by Richard Perceval Graves. Providence and Oxford: Berghahn Books, 1995. First pub., London: Cape, 1929. Rev. ed., New York: Doubleday, 1957.

———. *Hercules, My Shipmate.* New York: Creative Age, 1945.

———. *I, Claudius.* New York: Grosset and Dunlop, 1934.

———. *John Skelton (Laureate).* Augustan Books of English Poetry. London: Benn, 1927.

———. *King Jesus.* New York: Farrar, Straus and Company, 1946.

———. *Lawrence and the Arabs.* New York: Doubleday, 1928.

———. Letter to Frank Kersnowski dated Easter Sunday [1969].

———. Letters to Edward Marsh. Berg Collection, New York Public Library.

———. Letter to Eric S. Pinker dated 25 March 1925. Harry Ransom Humanities Research Center, University of Texas at Austin.

———. Letters to Siegfried Sassoon. Berg Collection, New York Public Library.

———. *Mammon and the Black Goddess.* Garden City, N.Y.: Doubleday and Company, 1965.

———. *Man Does, Woman Is.* London: Cassell, 1964.

———. *The Marmosite's Miscellany.* (Under pseud. of John Doyle.) London: Hogarth Press, 1925.

———. *The Meaning of Dreams.* New York: Greenberg Publishers, 1925.

———. *Mock Beggar Hall.* London: Hogarth Press, 1923.

———. *My Head! My Head!* New York: Alfred A. Knopf, 1925.

———. *New Poems.* Garden City, N.Y.: Doubleday and Company, 1963.

———. *No More Ghosts.* London: Faber, 1940.

———. *On English Poetry: Being an Irregular Approach to the Psychology of This Art, from Evidence Mainly Subjective.* New York: Alfred Knopf, 1922.

———. *Over the Brazier.* London: Poetry Bookshop, 1916.

———. *The Pier-Glass.* New York: Alfred Knopf, 1921.

———. *Poems (1914–1926).* London: Heinemann, 1927.

———. *Poetic Unreason and Other Studies.* London: Cecil Palmer, 1925.

———. *The Rubaiyat of Omar Khayaam: A New Translation with Critical Commentaries by Robert Graves and Omar Ali-Shah.* London: Cassell, 1968.

———. *The Shout*. London: Elkin Mathews & Marot, 1929.

———. "Sullen Moods" manuscripts. Poetry and Rare Book Collection, State University of New York at Buffalo.

———. *A Survey of Modernist Poetry*. (With Laura Riding.) London: Heinemann, 1928.

———. *To Return To All That*. London: Jonathan Cape, 1930.

———. *Treasure Box*. London: Chiswick Press, 1919.

———. *Watch the North Wind Rise*. New York: Creative Age, 1949.

———. *Welchman's Hose*. London: Fleuron, 1925.

———. *Whipperginny*. New York: Alfred Knopf, 1923.

———. *The White Goddess: A Historical Grammar of Poetic Myth*. Edited by Grevel Lindop. Manchester: Carcanet, 1997. First edition. London: Faber, 1948. The amended and enlarged edition has a different and very useful index. London: Faber and Faber, 1961.

Head, Henry. Letter to Robert Graves dated 7 April 1925. Harry Ransom Humanities Research Center, University of Texas at Austin.

Hemingway, Ernest. *A Farewell To Arms*. New York: Scribner's, 1943.

Higginson, Fred H. *A Bibliography of the Writings of Robert Graves*. 2d ed. Revised by William Proctor Williams. Winchester, Hampshire: St. Paul's Bibliographies, 1987.

Hulme, T. E. *Speculations: Essays on Humanism and the Philosophy of Art*. London: Routledge and Paul, 1936.

Joyce, James. *Ulysses*. New York: Modern Library, 1946.

Jung, Carl Gustav. Letter to Lawrence Durrell dated 15 December 1947. Special Collections, Morris Library, Southern Illinois University.

Keats, John. *Complete Poems*. Edited by Jack Stillinger. Cambridge and London: Belknap Press of Harvard University Press, 1982.

Keegan, John. *The Face of Battle: A Study of Againcourt, Waterloo, and the Somme*. New York: Viking, 1989.

Marsh, Edward, ed. *Georgian Poetry 1911–1912*. London: The Poetry Bookshop, 1912.

Matthews, T. S. *Under the Influence*. London: Cassell, 1977.

Owen, Wilfred. *The Complete Poems and Fragments*. Edited, with an introduction, by Jon Stallworthy. London: Chatto and Windus, 1983.

Palmer, H. E. "Robert Graves at World's End." Unpublished essay. Harry Ransom Humanities Research Center, University of Texas at Austin.

Quinn, Patrick. *The Great War and the Missing Muse: The Early Writings of Robert Graves and Siegfried Sassoon*. Selinsgrove: Susquehanna, 1994.

Rivers, W. H. R. *Conflict and Dream*. New York: Harcourt Brace, 1923.

Robbins, Rossell Hope. *The T. S. Eliot Myth*. New York: H. Schuman, 1951.

Sassoon, Siegfried. *Collected Poems*. London: Faber, 1987.

———. *Complete Memoirs of George Sherston*. New York: Literary Guild, 1937.

———. *Siegfried Sassoon Diaries, 1915–1918*. London: Faber and Faber, 1983.

Scarry, Elaine. *The Body in Pain*. New York and Oxford: Oxford, 1985.

Seymour, Miranda. *Robert Graves: Life on the Edge*. New York: Henry Holt, 1995.

Seymour-Smith, Martin. *Robert Graves: His Life and Work*. New York: Holt, Rinehart, and Winston, 1982.

Steiner, George. "The Genius of Robert Graves." *The Kenyon Review* 22:3 (summer 1960): 340–365.

Thomas, Sue. "Virginia Woolf's Septimus and Contemporary Perceptions of Shell Shock." *ELN* 25:2 (December 1987): 49–57.

Vickery, John B. *Robert Graves and the White Goddess*. Lincoln: University of Nebraska Press, 1972.

Yeats, William Butler. *Collected Poems*. London: Macmillan, 1958.

INDEX

Printed and bound by CPI Group (UK) Ltd, Croydon, CR0 4YY

13/04/2025

14656491-0002